Woodview Resource Library
Burlin
W9-CNJ-453

Sylvan Learning℠

At Sylvan, we believe anyone can master math skills and develop a love of reading, and we are glad you have chosen our resources to help your children experience the joy of both subjects as they build crucial reasoning skills. We know that time spent reinforcing lessons learned in school will contribute to understanding and mastery.

Reading comprehension is the foundation of success in all aspects of second-grade academics. As a successful reader, you hold infinite possibilities in your hands, enabling you to learn about anything and everything. Similarly, success in math requires more than just memorizing basic facts and algorithms; it also requires children to make connections between the real world and math concepts in order to solve problems. Successful problem solvers will be ready for the challenges of mathematics as they advance to more complex topics and encounter new problems both in school and at home.

We use a research-based, step-by-step process in teaching both reading and math that includes thought-provoking reading selections, math problems, and activities. The learning process also relies on high standards and meaningful parental involvement. With success, students feel increasing confidence. With increasing confidence, students build even more success. It's a perfect cycle. That's why our Sylvan workbooks aren't like the others. We're laying out the roadmap for learning that is designed to lead your child to success in school.

Included with your purchase of this workbook is a coupon for a discount at a participating Sylvan center. We hope you will use this coupon to further your children's academic journeys. Let us partner with you to support the development of confident, well-prepared, independent learners.

The Sylvan Team

Sylvan Learning℠

2nd Grade Basic Math Success

Contents

Place Value & Number Sense

1 Place Value 126
2 Number Lines & Patterns 132
3 Comparing Numbers 138
4 Rounding & Estimating 142
Review 146

Addition & Subtraction

5 Adding 150
6 Subtracting 154
7 Adding with Regrouping 158
8 Subtracting with Regrouping 162
Review 166

Grouping & Sharing

9 Grouping 170
10 Sharing Equally 174
11 Odd & Even 178
Review 180

Fractions

12 Recognizing Fractions 182
13 Comparing Fractions 186
Review 190

Measurement

14 Nonstandard Units 192
15 Inches 196
16 Centimeters 200
17 Perimeter & Area 204
Review 208

Time

18 Hours & Half Hours 212
19 Quarter Hours 216
20 It's about Time 220
21 Calendars 224
Review 228

Money

22 Money Values 230
23 Using Money 234
24 Comparing Amounts 238
Review 240
Answers 243

Get in Place

WRITE how many tens and ones you see. Then WRITE the number they make.

1.

Tens	Ones
5	3

= 53

2.

Tens	Ones

=

3.

Tens	Ones

=

4.

Tens	Ones

=

5.

Tens	Ones

=

6.

Tens	Ones

=

7.

Tens	Ones

=

8.

Tens	Ones

=

Get in Place

WRITE how many tens and ones you see.
Then WRITE the number they make.

1.

Tens	Ones

=

2.

Tens	Ones

=

3.

Tens	Ones

=

4.

Tens	Ones

=

5.

Tens	Ones

=

6.

Tens	Ones

=

7.

Tens	Ones

=

8.

Tens	Ones

=

Get in Place

WRITE how many hundreds, tens, and ones you see. Then WRITE the number they make.

1.

Hundreds	Tens	Ones

=

2.

Hundreds	Tens	Ones

=

3.

Hundreds	Tens	Ones

=

4.

Hundreds	Tens	Ones

=

5.

Hundreds	Tens	Ones

=

Number Match

CIRCLE the picture in each row that matches the number.

219

571

458

844

390

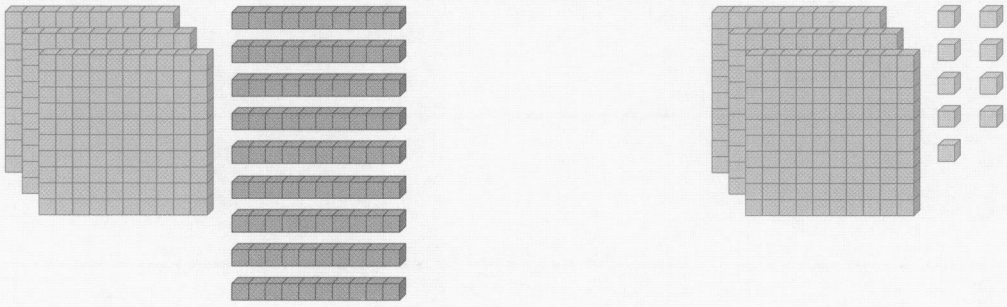

Write the Number

WRITE the number words.

HINT: Remember to put a hyphen in numbers connecting the tens and ones, like seventy-four or thirty-three.

1 one	11 eleven	30 thirty
2 two	12 twelve	40 forty
3 three	13 thirteen	50 fifty
4 four	14 fourteen	60 sixty
5 five	15 fifteen	70 seventy
6 six	16 sixteen	80 eighty
7 seven	17 seventeen	90 ninety
8 eight	18 eighteen	100 one hundred
9 nine	19 nineteen	
10 ten	20 twenty	

1. 162 one hundred sixty-two

2. 374 _____

3. 250 _____

4. 816 _____

5. 643 _____

6. 495 _____

Match Up

DRAW lines to connect the numbers and words that go together.

589	two hundred eleven
108	three hundred twenty-eight
328	seven hundred thirty-four
947	nine hundred forty-seven
211	five hundred eighty-nine
734	one hundred eight

Holey Hundreds!

WRITE the missing numbers on the chart. Then COLOR the chart by following the directions on the next page.

1	2		4	5	6	7	8		10
	12	13	14		16	17	18	19	20
21	22	23		25	26		28	29	30
31	32	33	34	35		37	38	39	40
41		43	44	45	46	47	48	49	50
51	52	53	54		56	57	58		60
	62	63	64	65	66	67	68	69	
71	72	73		75	76		78	79	80
81	82	83	84	85	86	87	88	89	90
91		93	94	95	96	97		99	100

1. COLOR number 33 blue.
2. COLOR number 57 red.
3. COLOR number 94 purple.
4. COLOR number 52 orange.

5. COLOR the number that is 2 more than 7 blue.
6. COLOR the number that is 8 more than 17 red.
7. COLOR the number that is 10 less than 71 purple.
8. COLOR the number that is 16 less than 56 orange.

9. Starting at number 8, SKIP COUNT by 10 and COLOR the squares yellow.
10. Starting at number 75, SKIP COUNT by 5 and COLOR the squares green.

1	2		4	5	6	7	8		10
	12	13	14		16	17	18	19	20
21	22	23		25	26		28	29	30
31	32	[illegible]	34	35		37	38	39	40
41		43	44	45	46	47	48	49	50
51	[illegible]	53	54		56	57	58		60
	62	63	64	65	66	67	68	69	
71	72	73		75	76		78	79	80
81	82	83	84	85	86	87	88	89	90
91		93	94	95	96	97		99	100

Pattern Patch

WRITE the missing numbers in the boxes.

82	83	84		86	87		89

103			106	107		109	

	344	345		347			350

719	720						

566							573

						856	857

Get in Line

WRITE the missing numbers on each number line.

234 235 236 237 ___ 239 240 ___

___ 982 983 ___ ___ 986 ___ 988

97 ___ ___ ___ 101 ___ 103 ___

874 875 ___ ___ ___ ___ ___ ___

699 ___ ___ ___ ___ ___ ___ 706

___ ___ ___ ___ ___ ___ 401 402

Get in Line

SKIP COUNT and WRITE the missing numbers on each number line.

Skip count by 2:

+2

2 4 6 8

Skip count by 5:

50 55 60

Skip count by 10:

60 70 80

Skip count by 3:

15 18 21

Skip count by 8:

8 16 24

Skip count by 6:

42 48 54

Pattern Patch

DETERMINE what number is being used for skip counting. Then WRITE the rest of the pattern.

66	68	70					

20	30	40					

15	20	25					

27	30	33					

62	66	70					

42	49	56					

Which One?

CIRCLE the picture in each pair that has **more** than the other.

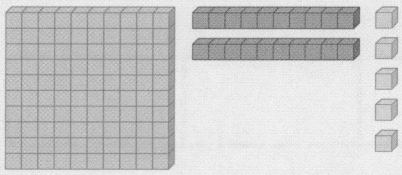

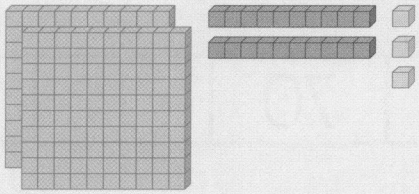

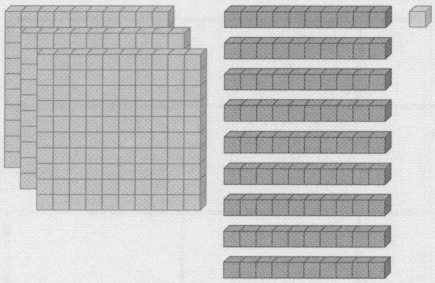

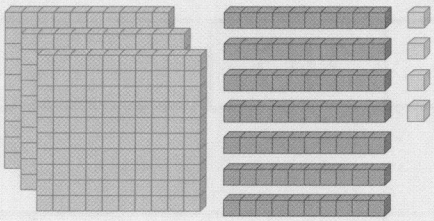

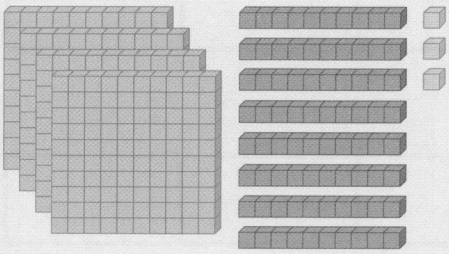

Circle It

CIRCLE the number that is **less** than the number shown in the picture.

1. 

576 600

2. 

329 340

3. 

713 707

4. 

458 464

5. 

915 910

Mismatched

WRITE > or < in each box.

3 : 8 First, draw two dots next to the larger number.

3 · : 8 Next, draw one dot next to the smaller number.

3 < 8 Then, connect the dots.

7 < 12 (1)	34 ☐ 29 (2)	60 ☐ 70 (3)
55 ☐ 51 (4)	82 ☐ 91 (5)	36 ☐ 63 (6)
109 ☐ 101 (7)	872 ☐ 882 (8)	528 ☐ 519 (9)
249 ☐ 224 (10)	450 ☐ 339 (11)	695 ☐ 729 (12)
366 ☐ 386 (13)	910 ☐ 889 (14)	731 ☐ 741 (15)
406 ☐ 399 (16)	298 ☐ 300 (17)	671 ☐ 617 (18)

Matched or Mismatched?

WRITE >, <, or = in each box.

HINT: Use = when numbers are the same.

112 > 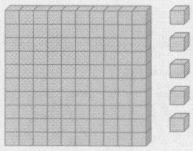

1

247 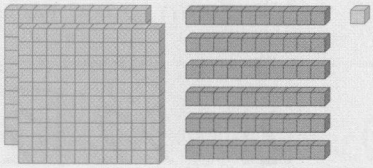

2

735 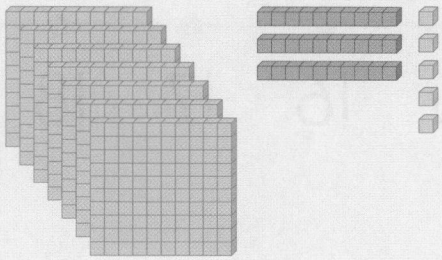

3

490 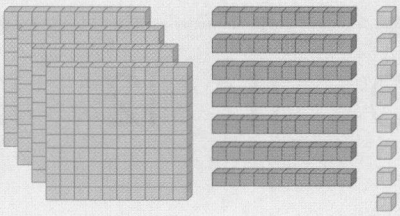

4

599 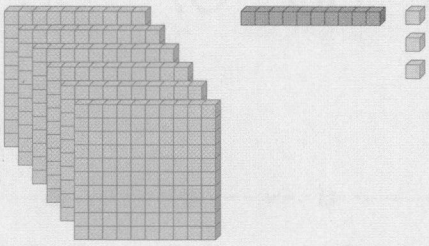

5

103 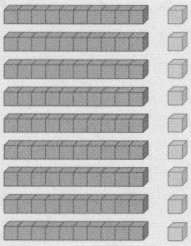

6

381 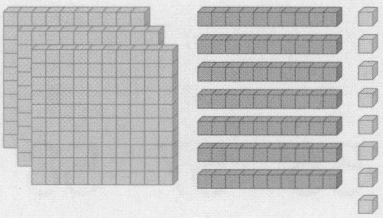

7

227 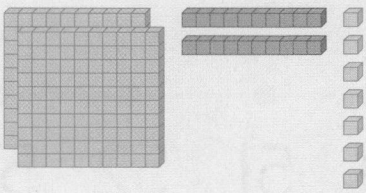

8

Round About

Rounding makes numbers easier to use.

Numbers that end in 1 through 4 get rounded **down** to the nearest ten.

Numbers that end in 5 through 9 get rounded **up** to the nearest ten.

ROUND each red number to the nearest ten.

1 2

3 4

5 6

7 8

Round About

Numbers that end in 1 through 49 get rounded **down** to the nearest hundred.

Numbers that end in 50 through 99 get rounded **up** to the nearest hundred.

ROUND each number to the nearest hundred.

1. 689
2. 906
3. 415
4. 279
5. 538
6. 391
7. 155
8. 748
9. 332
10. 873
11. 650
12. 942

Guess and Check

Estimating is making a reasonable guess about something. GUESS the number of cubes in each set, then CHECK your guess by counting the cubes.

1.

Guess:

Check:

2.

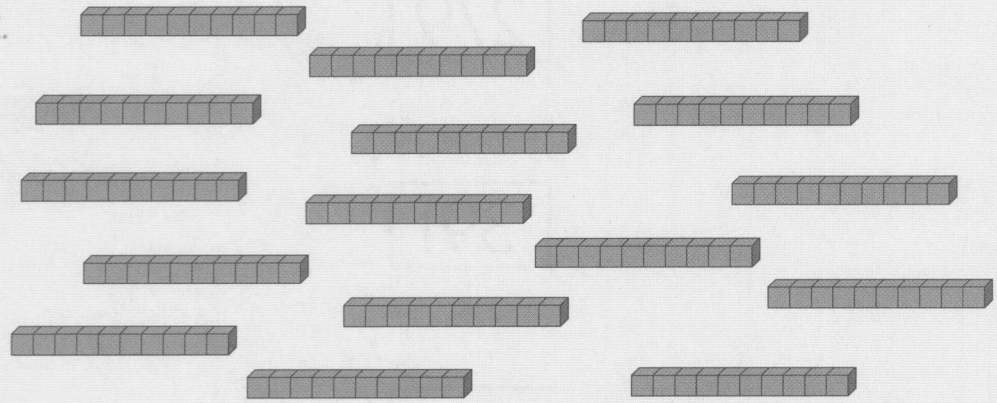

Guess:

Check:

3.

Guess:

Check:

Loop It

GUESS the number of bugs. Then CIRCLE groups of five to count the bugs and check your guess.

1.

Guess:

Check:

2.

Guess:

Check:

3.

Guess:

Check:

Write the Number

WRITE the number and the number words for each picture.

1.

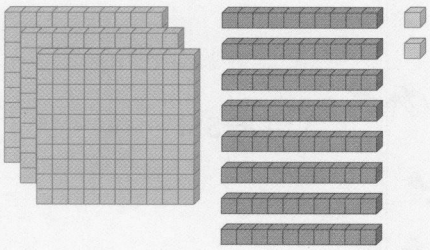

2.

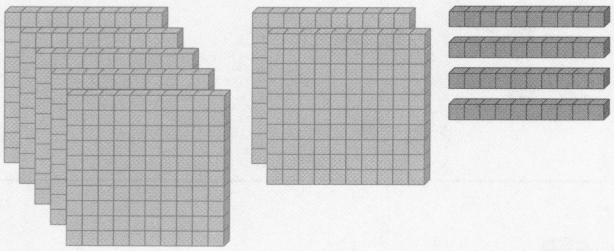

3.

4.

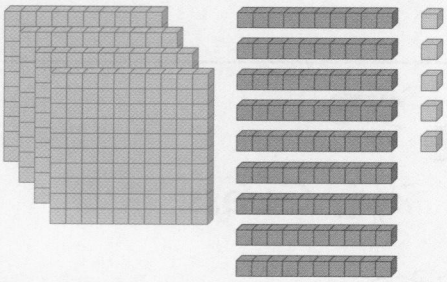

5.

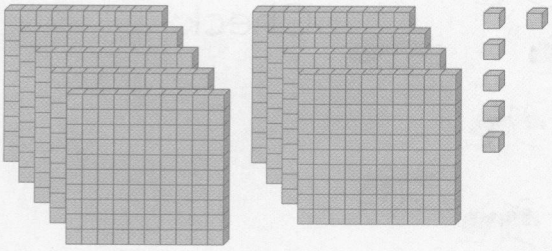

Get in Line

WRITE the missing numbers on each number line.

245 246 ☐ ☐ ☐ ☐ ☐ ☐

589 ☐ ☐ ☐ ☐ ☐ ☐ 596

☐ ☐ ☐ ☐ ☐ ☐ 730 731

WRITE the missing numbers to finish each pattern.

40	45	50					

26	29	32					

11	17	23					

Matched or Mismatched?

WRITE >, <, or = in each box.

1.

2.

3.

4. 588 ☐ 577

5. 120 ☐ 135

6. 311 ☐ 311

7. 271 ☐ 274

8. 999 ☐ 989

9. 759 ☐ 763

Round About

ROUND each number to the nearest ten.

88 ____ 1

31 ____ 2

44 ____ 3

57 ____ 4

12 ____ 5

95 ____ 6

7 ____ 7

15 ____ 8

ROUND each number to the nearest hundred.

604 ____ 9

178 ____ 10

497 ____ 11

739 ____ 12

218 ____ 13

360 ____ 14

852 ____ 15

243 ____ 16

Guess and Check

GUESS the number of jellybeans. Then CIRCLE groups of five to count the jellybeans and check your guess.

Guess: ____

Check: ____ 17

Picture It

WRITE each sum.

52
+ 34
86 8 tens, 6 ones

1. 31
+ 25

2. 17
+ 12

3. 11
+ 67

4. 24
+ 20

5. 46
+ 22

6. 33
+ 36

Cash Crunch

WRITE each sum.

1. 

21¢ + 41¢ = ____ ¢

2. 

81¢ + 15¢ = ____ ¢

3. 

23¢ + 21¢ = ____ ¢

4. 

57¢ + 32¢ = ____ ¢

5. 

33¢ + 24¢ = ____ ¢

6. 

27¢ + 52¢ = ____ ¢

It All Adds Up

WRITE each sum.

1. 62 + 17 =

2. 13 + 41 =

3. 88 + 10 =

4. 55 + 32 =

5. 22 + 22 =

6. 20 + 19 =

7. 64 + 12 =

8. 43 + 26 =

9. 44 + 33 =

10. 30 + 18 =

11. 10 + 21 =

12. 25 + 72 =

13. 18 + 41 =

14. 80 + 14 =

15. 32 + 32 =

16. 54 + 35 =

It All Adds Up

WRITE each missing number.

1. 65 + ___ = 75

2. 38 + ___ = 59

3. 14 + ___ = 26

4. 53 + ___ = 98

5. 41 + ___ = 83

6. 11 + ___ = 76

7. 25 + ___ = 97

8. 70 + ___ = 88

9. ___ + 77 = 99

10. 50 + ___ = 63

11. 31 + ___ = 82

12. ___ + 16 = 59

13. ___ + 40 = 72

14. 64 + ___ = 95

15. 12 + ___ = 34

16. ___ + 81 = 93

Picture It

WRITE each difference.

37
− 12
25 2 tens, 5 ones

1. 74
− 31

2. 58
− 26

3. 95
− 43

4. 89
− 64

5. 35
− 22

6. 77
− 16

Cash Crunch

WRITE each difference.

HINT: Cross out dimes and pennies to help you subtract.

1.

48¢ – 13¢ = 35 ¢

2.

64¢ – 33¢ = ¢

3.

81¢ – 21¢ = ¢

4.

38¢ – 26¢ = ¢

5.

99¢ – 73¢ = ¢

6.

83¢ – 42¢ = ¢

What's the Difference?

WRITE each difference.

1. 59 − 32 =
2. 36 − 26 =
3. 62 − 41 =
4. 87 − 75 =
5. 91 − 10 =
6. 48 − 23 =
7. 76 − 14 =
8. 58 − 45 =
9. 60 − 20 =
10. 39 − 28 =
11. 46 − 16 =
12. 55 − 31 =
13. 73 − 21 =
14. 28 − 13 =
15. 95 − 23 =
16. 88 − 57 =

What's the Difference?

WRITE each missing number.

1. 90 − ☐ = 40
2. 79 − ☐ = 33
3. 24 − ☐ = 12
4. 56 − ☐ = 41
5. 63 − ☐ = 22
6. 85 − ☐ = 65
7. 37 − ☐ = 10
8. 92 − ☐ = 71
9. ☐ − 23 = 72
10. 45 − ☐ = 11
11. 83 − ☐ = 53
12. ☐ − 19 = 50
13. ☐ − 11 = 64
14. 68 − ☐ = 44
15. 78 − ☐ = 21
16. ☐ − 32 = 16

Picture It

WRITE each sum.

26
+ 45

6 tens, 11 ones

71 7 tens, 1 one

11 ones = 1 ten, 1 one

1. 19
+ 23

2. 56
+ 37

3. 48
+ 34

4. 36
+ 29

5. 78
+ 13

6. 53
+ 17

Cash Crunch

WRITE each sum.

HINT: Remember that the value of ten pennies equals one dime.

1. 16¢ + 49¢ = ____ ¢

2. 74¢ + 18¢ = ____ ¢

3. 29¢ + 41¢ = ____ ¢

4. 35¢ + 46¢ = ____ ¢

5. 25¢ + 27¢ = ____ ¢

6. 58¢ + 15¢ = ____ ¢

It All Adds Up

WRITE each sum.

$\begin{array}{r} 29 \\ +13 \\ \hline \end{array}$ First, add the numbers in the ones place. 9 + 3 = 12	$\begin{array}{r} {}^{1} \\ 29 \\ +13 \\ \hline 2 \end{array}$ Write a 2 in the ones place, and write a 1 in the tens place.	$\begin{array}{r} {}^{1} \\ 29 \\ +13 \\ \hline 42 \end{array}$ Then add the tens. 1 + 2 + 1 = 4. Write 4 in the tens place. 29 + 13 = 42

1. $\begin{array}{r} 26 \\ +35 \\ \hline \end{array}$

2. $\begin{array}{r} 62 \\ +19 \\ \hline \end{array}$

3. $\begin{array}{r} 75 \\ +15 \\ \hline \end{array}$

4. $\begin{array}{r} 37 \\ +54 \\ \hline \end{array}$

5. $\begin{array}{r} 48 \\ +22 \\ \hline \end{array}$

6. $\begin{array}{r} 37 \\ +37 \\ \hline \end{array}$

7. $\begin{array}{r} 17 \\ +18 \\ \hline \end{array}$

8. $\begin{array}{r} 39 \\ +19 \\ \hline \end{array}$

9. $\begin{array}{r} 16 \\ +16 \\ \hline \end{array}$

10. $\begin{array}{r} 66 \\ +14 \\ \hline \end{array}$

11. $\begin{array}{r} 28 \\ +38 \\ \hline \end{array}$

12. $\begin{array}{r} 58 \\ +34 \\ \hline \end{array}$

It All Adds Up

WRITE each sum.

1. 47 + 13 = ____
2. 18 + 57 = ____
3. 24 + 68 = ____
4. 48 + 19 = ____
5. 36 + 54 = ____
6. 27 + 14 = ____
7. 49 + 33 = ____
8. 11 + 39 = ____
9. 54 + 17 = ____
10. 35 + 29 = ____
11. 79 + 21 = ____
12. 48 + 47 = ____

Picture It

WRITE each difference.

42
− 15

27 2 tens, 7 ones

1. 93
− 26

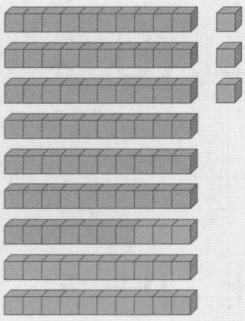

2. 70
− 54

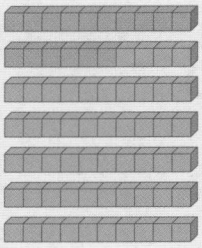

3. 76
− 37

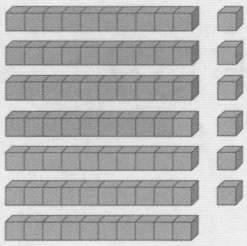

4. 81
− 8

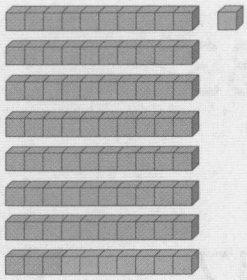

5. 66
− 48

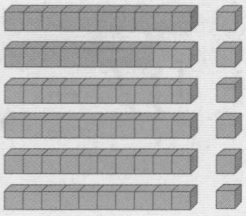

6. 52
− 25

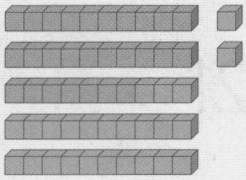

Picture It

WRITE each difference.

HINT: Color the number of cubes being subtracted, then count the number of cubes remaining.

1. 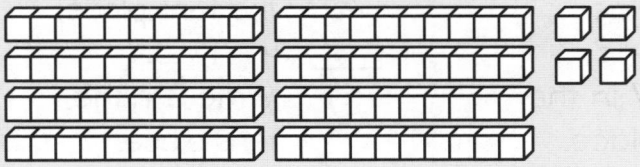

84 – 56 =

2. 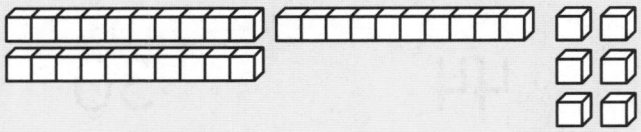

36 – 18 =

3. 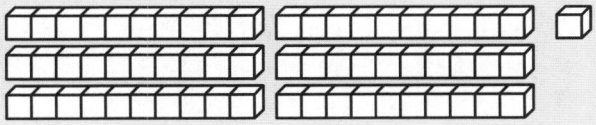

61 – 22 =

4. 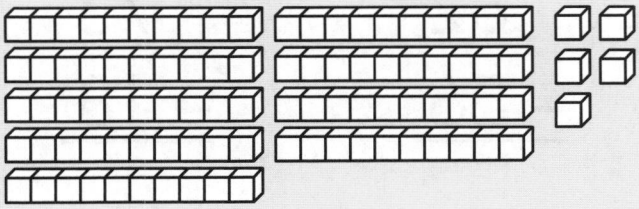

95 – 29 =

5. 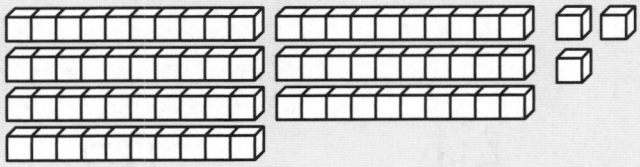

73 – 58 =

6. 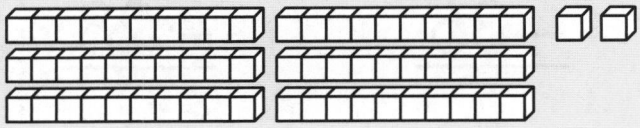

62 – 5 =

What's the Difference?

WRITE each difference.

53 −16	First, regroup from the tens place. Cross out the 5 and write 4, and cross out the 3 and write 13.	4 13 ~~5~~~~3~~ −16 7	Subtract in the ones place: 13 − 6 = 7. Write 7 in the ones place.	4 13 ~~5~~~~3~~ −16 37	Then, subtract in the tens place: 4 − 1 = 3. Write 3 in the tens place. 53 − 16 = 37

1. 78 − 19 =

2. 35 − 27 =

3. 44 − 15 =

4. 30 − 12 =

5. 85 − 47 =

6. 93 − 68 =

7. 82 − 56 =

8. 73 − 18 =

9. 63 − 26 =

10. 95 − 86 =

11. 64 − 36 =

12. 47 − 28 =

What's the Difference?

WRITE each difference.

1. 52 – 35 =
2. 61 – 57 =
3. 98 – 19 =
4. 74 – 17 =
5. 47 – 28 =
6. 51 – 13 =
7. 41 – 18 =
8. 80 – 39 =
9. 65 – 26 =
10. 72 – 25 =
11. 90 – 16 =
12. 54 – 45 =

Work It Out

Hector is deciding which two things to buy at the Eddie's Electronics store. He sees a video game for 31 dollars, a DVD for 25 dollars, a game controller for 15 dollars, a pack of batteries for 8 dollars, and headphones for 14 dollars.

WRITE the total cost of each of these possible purchases.

1. A pack of batteries and headphones $ _____
2. A DVD and a game controller $ _____
3. Headphones and a video game $ _____
4. A game controller and a pack of batteries $ _____
5. A video game and a DVD $ _____
6. If Hector has $20 and buys headphones, how much money would he have left? $ _____

Work It Out

Betty and Joe love to eat hamburgers in the summertime. They ate 23 hamburgers in June, 26 hamburgers in July, and 18 hamburgers in August.

1. How many total hamburgers did Betty and Joe eat in June and July? _____
2. How many total hamburgers did they eat in July and August? _____
3. If Joe ate 15 hamburgers in June, how many did Betty eat that month? _____
4. If Betty ate 14 hamburgers in July, how many did Joe eat that month? _____

Unit Rewind

WRITE each missing number.

1. ☐ + 28 = 89
2. 13 + ☐ = 54
3. 45 + ☐ = 65
4. ☐ + 32 = 48
5. ☐ + 20 = 99
6. 61 + ☐ = 83
7. 77 − ☐ = 33
8. ☐ − 16 = 40
9. ☐ − 35 = 54
10. 97 − ☐ = 46
11. 39 − ☐ = 24
12. ☐ − 15 = 72

Unit Rewind

WRITE each sum or difference.

1. 14 + 44 = ____
2. 28 + 11 = ____
3. 72 + 23 = ____
4. 64 + 25 = ____
5. 39 + 52 = ____
6. 66 + 15 = ____
7. 58 + 17 = ____
8. 37 + 27 = ____
9. 74 − 32 = ____
10. 45 − 12 = ____
11. 99 − 49 = ____
12. 83 − 62 = ____
13. 63 − 47 = ____
14. 30 − 16 = ____
15. 87 − 39 = ____
16. 51 − 22 = ____

Pick a Package

How many bags of five marbles can be made from the loose marbles? WRITE the answer.

HINT: Draw circles around groups of five, and count the number of groups you have.

bags

Pick a Package

Each seed packet comes with eight seeds. How many packets are needed to hold the seeds? How many seeds are there? WRITE the answers.

HINT: Draw circles around groups of eight, and use the groups to help you count the seeds.

seed packets for seeds

Pick a Package

How many of each type of box would be needed to pack the chocolates on the conveyor belt? WRITE the answer below each box.

1

2

3

4

Games Galore

WRITE the total number of game parts you see in the four games.

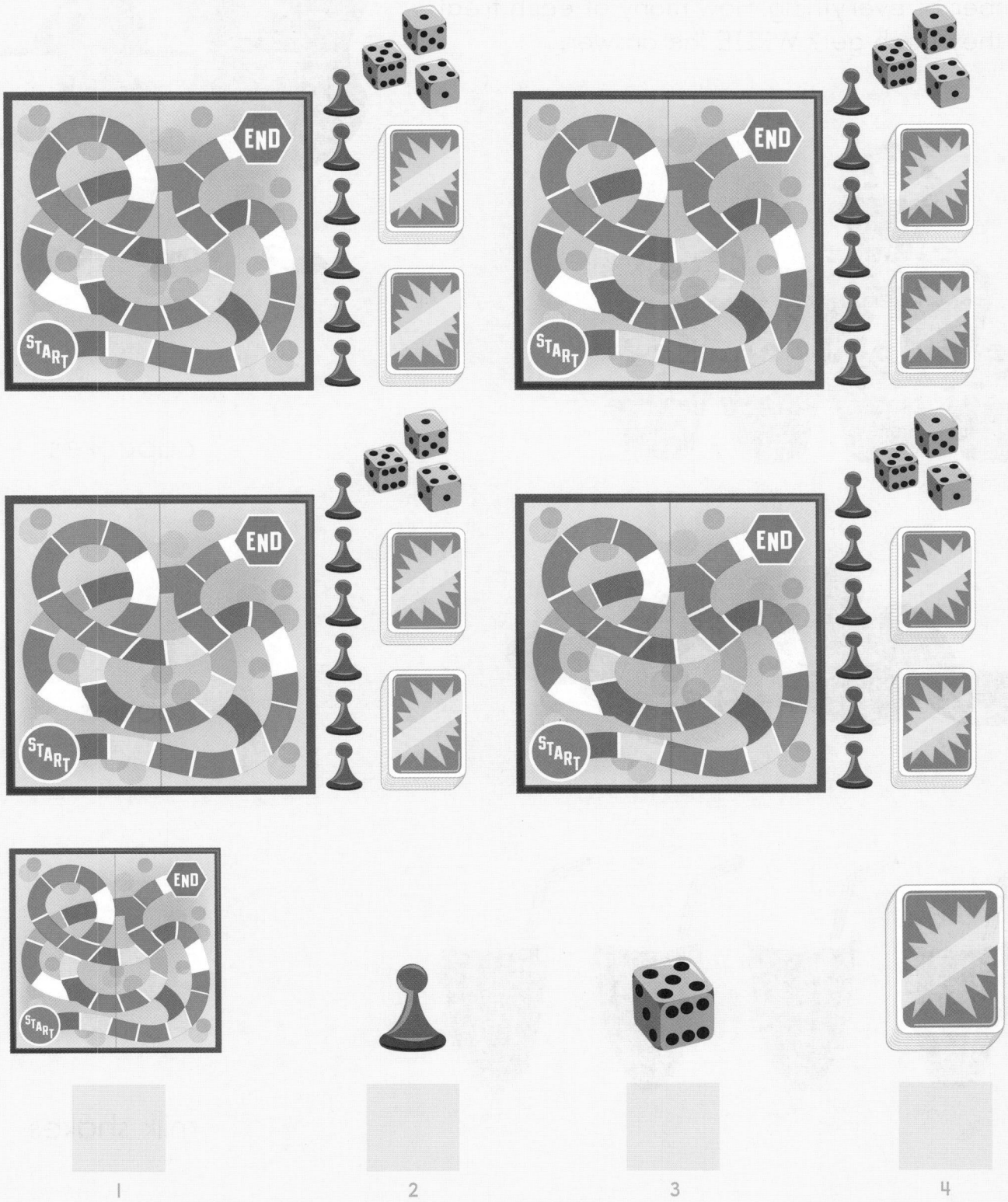

Fair Share

The twins aren't happy unless they get the same number of everything. How many of each treat will they each get? WRITE the answer.

cupcakes

1

cookies

2

milk shakes

3

Fair Share

If the same number of cards is dealt to every player, how many cards will each player get? WRITE the answer.

_____ cards

Fair Share

WRITE the number of gems each pirate will get if they split the treasure equally.

1

2

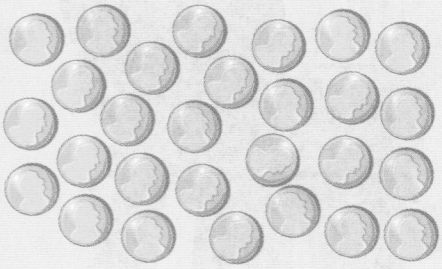

3

4

Fair Share

A family of five is having dinner, and everyone can eat the same amount of food. If each type of food is shared equally, how many pieces of each will a person get? How many pieces will be left over?
WRITE the answers.

1.

_____ piece of chicken _____ left over

2.

_____ French fries _____ left over

3.

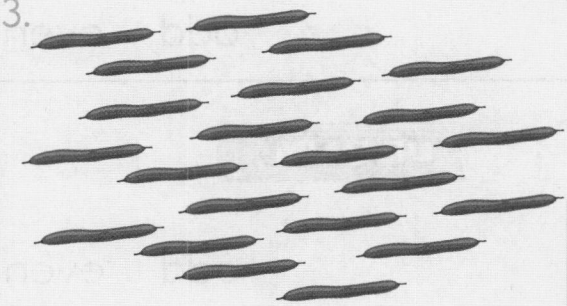

_____ green beans _____ left over

Odd or Even?

An even number of items can be shared equally by two people. An odd number of items cannot be shared equally by two people. There will always be one extra item. CIRCLE **odd** or **even** for each group.

1.

odd even

2.

odd even

3.

odd even

4.

odd even

5.

odd even

6.

odd even

Card Tricks

CIRCLE all of the cards with even numbers.

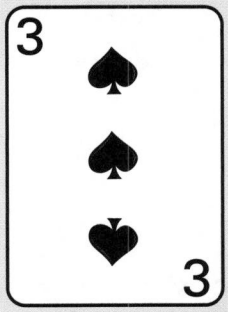

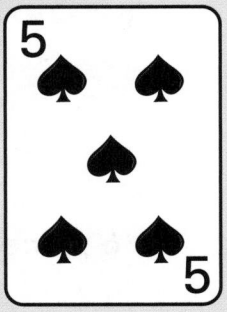

Pick a Package

How many of each bag would be needed to pack all of the candy? WRITE the answer.

1

2

3

4

5

Fair Share

WRITE the number of bananas each monkey will get when they are shared equally.

1. ☐ bananas

Odd or Even?

CIRCLE **odd** or **even**.

2. 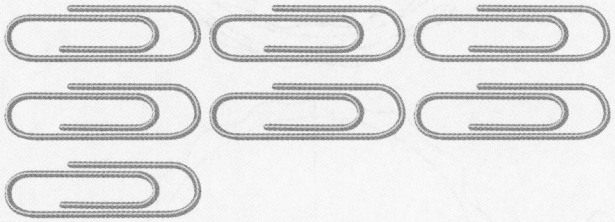

odd even

3. 

odd even

4. 

odd even

Piece of Cake

COLOR the cake pieces to match each fraction.

Example: $\frac{1}{4}$ ← colored piece ← pieces total

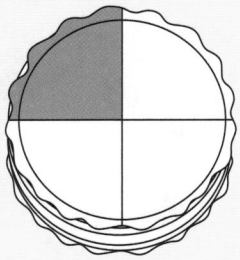

$\frac{1}{2}$

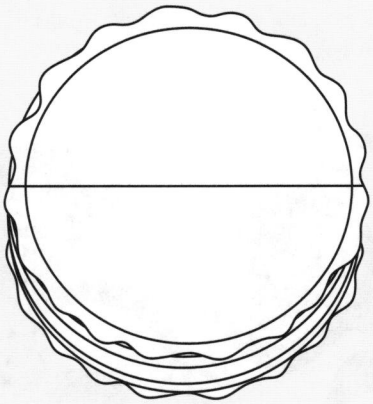

$\frac{1}{3}$

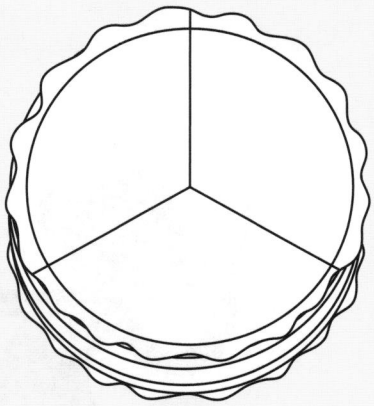

$\frac{2}{4}$

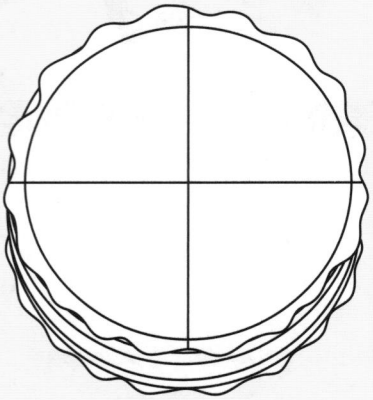

$\frac{2}{2}$

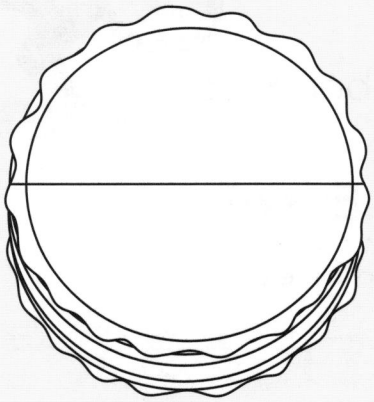

$\frac{2}{3}$

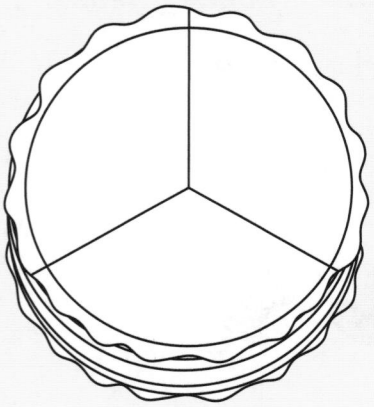

$\frac{3}{4}$

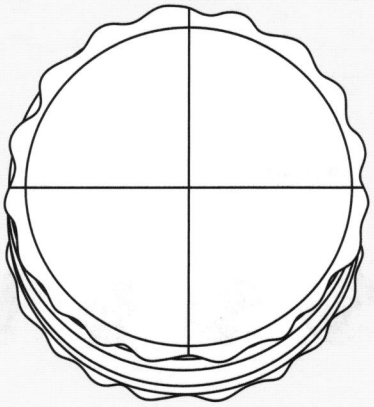

Fraction Bars

WRITE the fraction for each picture.

Example:

$\frac{2}{3}$ ← colored sections / ← total sections

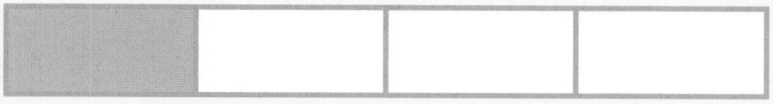

1 _____

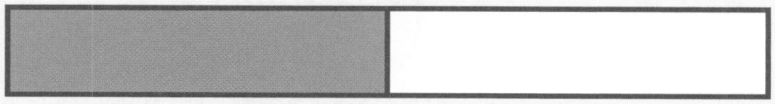

2 _____

3 _____

4 _____

5 _____

6 _____

Match Up

DRAW lines to connect the fractions and pictures that go together.

$\frac{2}{3}$

$\frac{1}{4}$

$\frac{1}{2}$

$\frac{3}{4}$

$\frac{1}{3}$

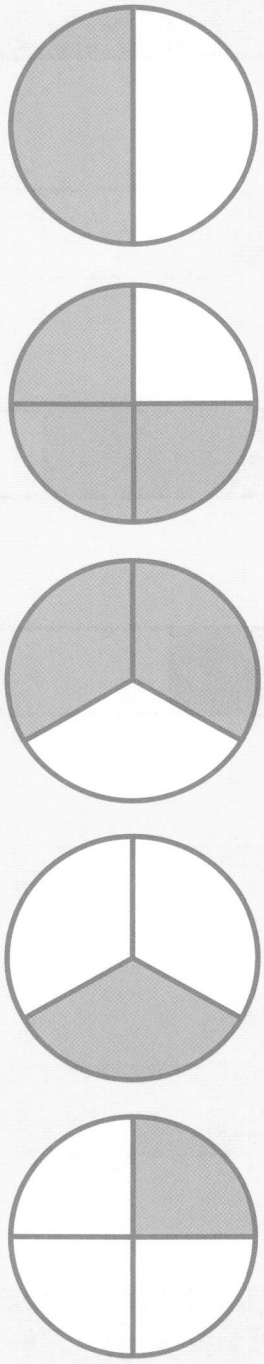

Color the Shapes

COLOR the part or parts of each shape to match the fraction.

$\frac{3}{4}$

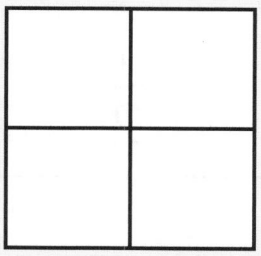

$\frac{2}{3}$

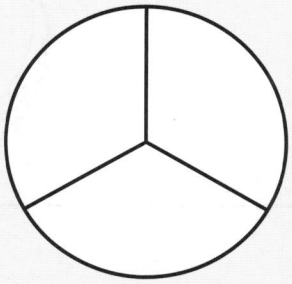

$\frac{1}{3}$

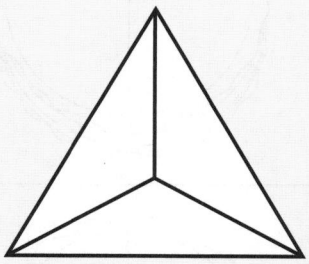

$\frac{1}{4}$

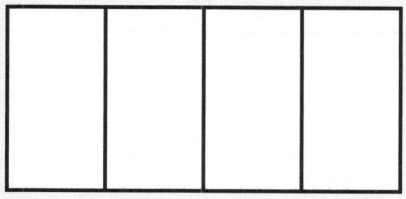

$\frac{1}{2}$

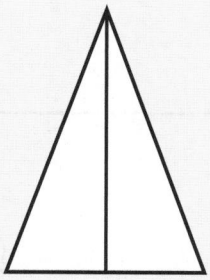

$\frac{4}{4}$

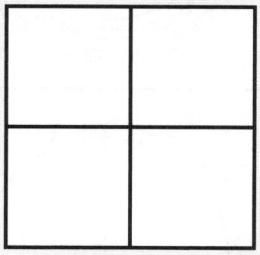

Piece of Cake

COLOR the cake pieces to match each fraction. Then CIRCLE the larger fraction.

HINT: The larger fraction is the one with more of the cake colored.

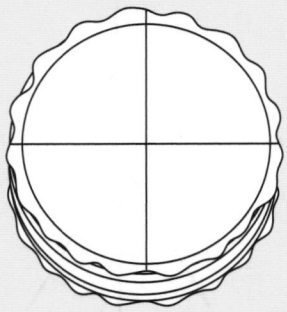

$\frac{1}{4}$

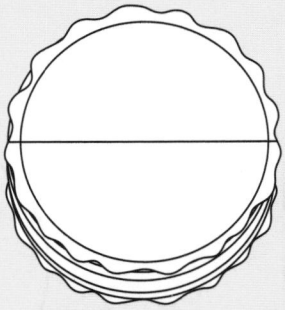

$\frac{1}{2}$

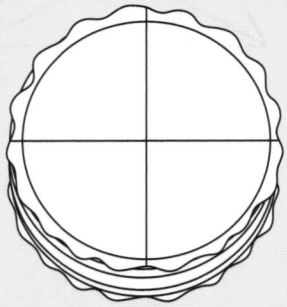

$\frac{2}{4}$

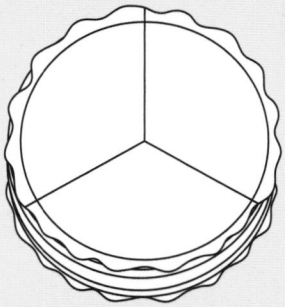

$\frac{2}{3}$

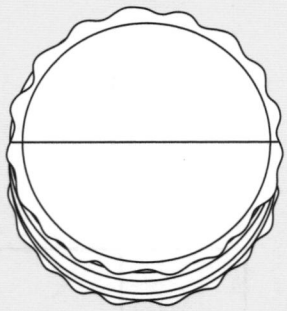

$\frac{1}{2}$

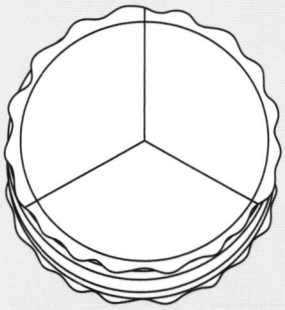

$\frac{1}{3}$

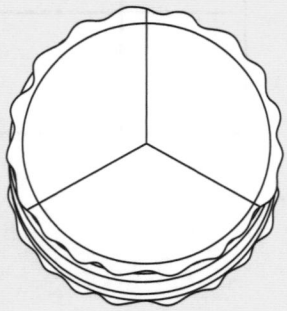

$\frac{2}{3}$

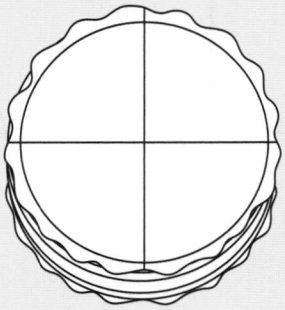

$\frac{3}{4}$

Fraction Bars

WRITE the fraction for each picture. Then CIRCLE the smaller fraction.

1.

_____ _____

2.

_____ _____

3.

_____ _____

4.

_____ _____

Pizza Party

DRAW a line to match each person to the correct slice of pizza.
Then WRITE answers to the questions.

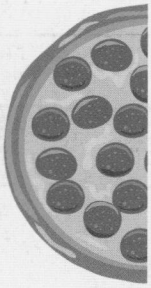

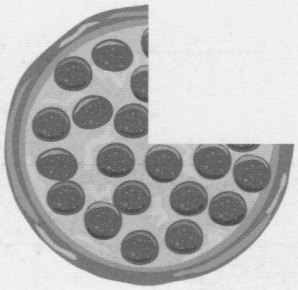

1. Who has the largest slice of pizza? _____

2. Who has the smallest slice of pizza? _____

Matched or Mismatched?

WRITE >, <, or = in each box.

HINT: Use these fraction circles to help you picture the fractions.

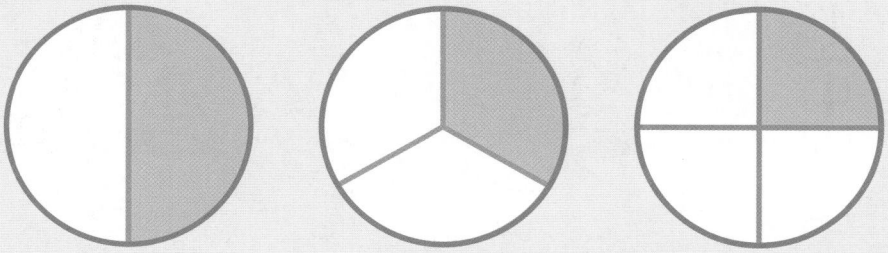

1. $\frac{1}{4}$ ☐ $\frac{1}{3}$
2. $\frac{2}{2}$ ☐ $\frac{2}{3}$
3. $\frac{2}{4}$ ☐ $\frac{1}{2}$
4. $\frac{3}{4}$ ☐ $\frac{1}{2}$
5. $\frac{1}{2}$ ☐ $\frac{1}{3}$
6. $\frac{3}{3}$ ☐ $\frac{3}{4}$
7. $\frac{1}{4}$ ☐ $\frac{1}{2}$
8. $\frac{4}{4}$ ☐ $\frac{3}{3}$
9. $\frac{1}{2}$ ☐ $\frac{2}{3}$
10. $\frac{2}{3}$ ☐ $\frac{2}{4}$
11. $\frac{3}{4}$ ☐ $\frac{1}{3}$
12. $\frac{2}{3}$ ☐ $\frac{3}{4}$

Match Up

DRAW lines to connect the fractions and pictures that go together.

$\frac{1}{4}$

$\frac{3}{4}$

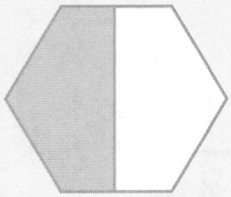

$\frac{2}{3}$

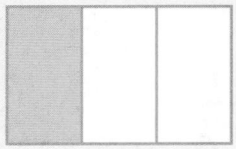

$\frac{1}{2}$

$\frac{1}{3}$

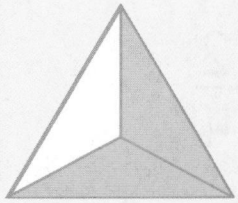

Fraction Bars

COLOR the fraction bars to match each fraction. Then WRITE >, <, or = in each box.

$\frac{1}{3}$ ☐ $\frac{1}{4}$

$\frac{2}{3}$ ☐ $\frac{3}{4}$

$\frac{2}{2}$ ☐ $\frac{4}{4}$

$\frac{1}{2}$ ☐ $\frac{1}{3}$

Measure Up

MEASURE the length of each object in paper clips.

1 paper clips

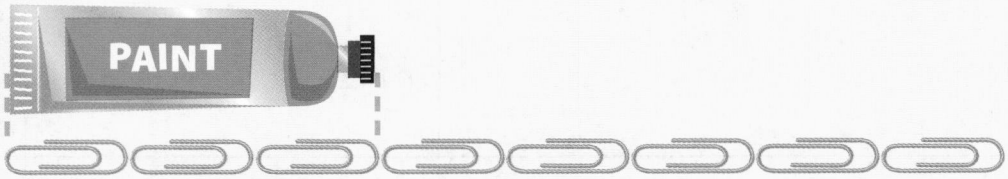

2 paper clips

3 paper clips

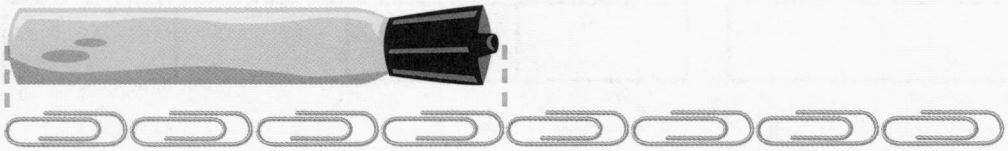

4 paper clips

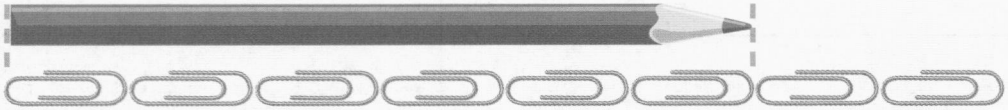

5 paper clips

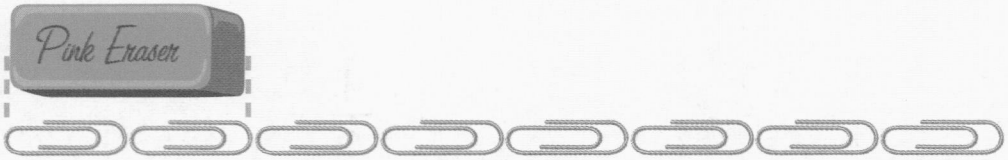

6 paper clips

Measure Up

MEASURE the length of each object in dimes.

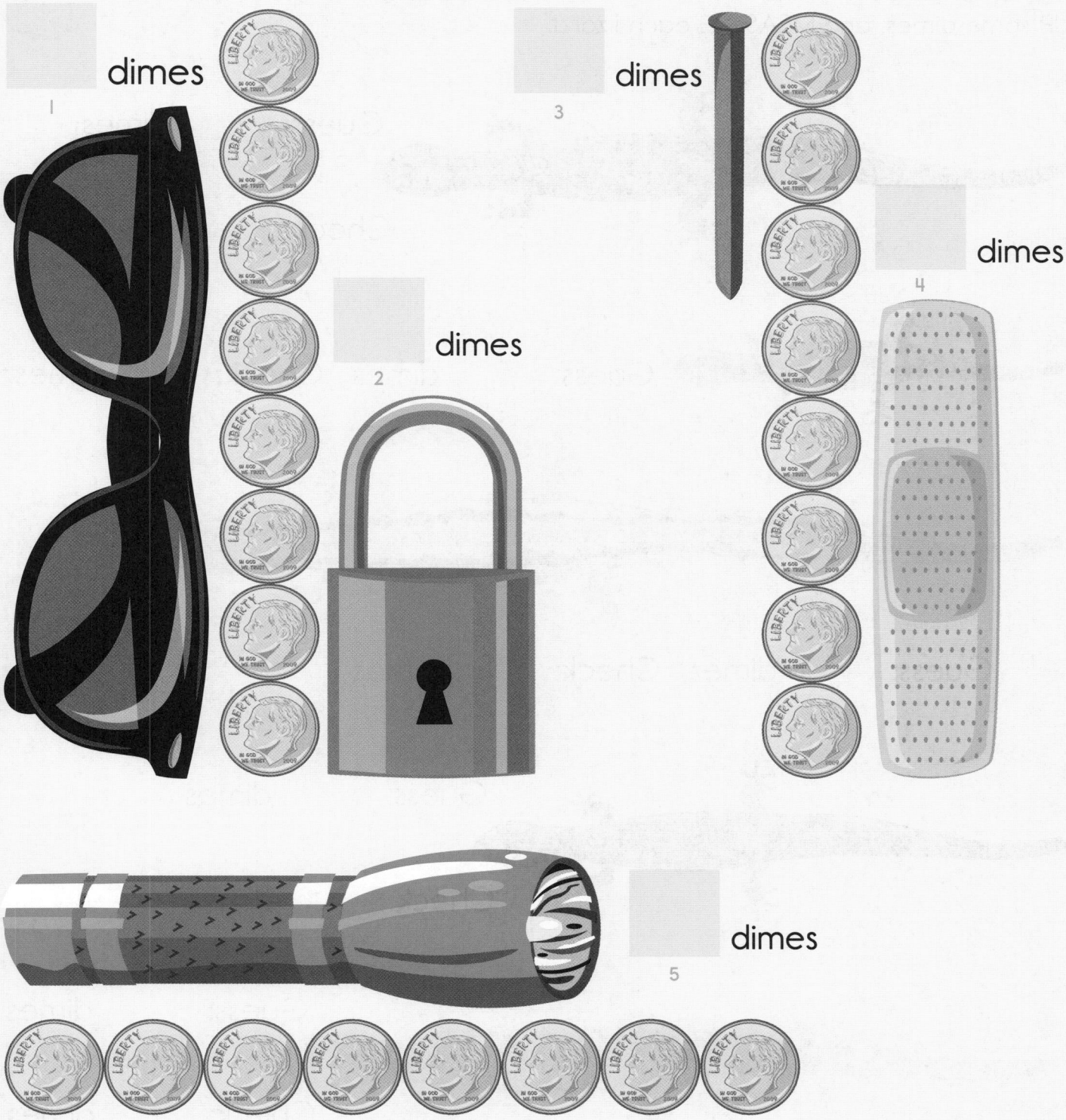

Dime Line

The lizard at the top is 5 dimes long. GUESS the length of each lizard in dimes. Then LINE UP some dimes, and MEASURE each lizard.

1.

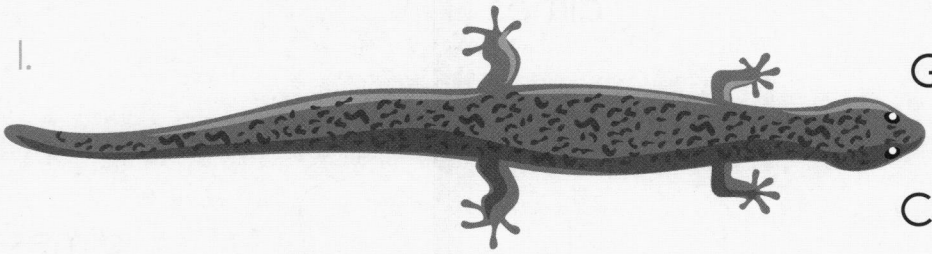

Guess: _____ dimes

Check: _____ dimes

2.

Guess: _____ dimes Check: _____ dimes

3.

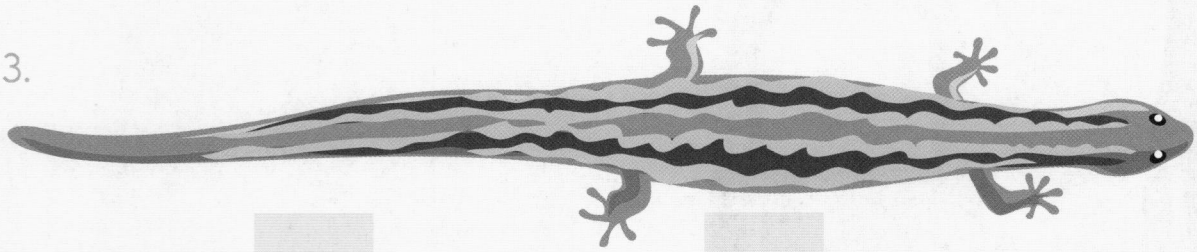

Guess: _____ dimes Check: _____ dimes

4.

Guess: _____ dimes

Check: _____ dimes

5.

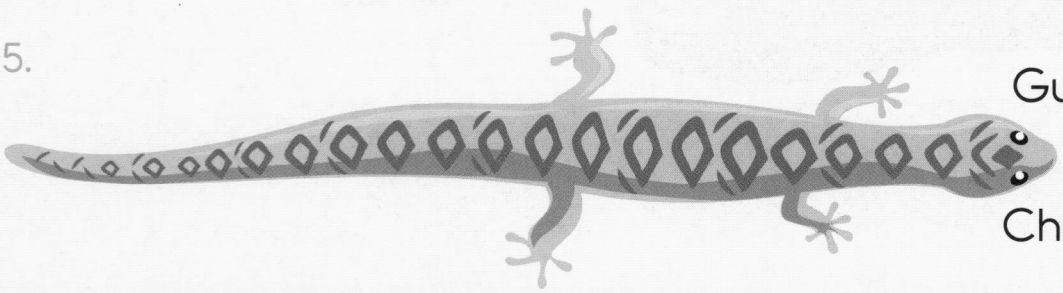

Guess: _____ dimes

Check: _____ dimes

Dime Line

Each piece of yarn needs to be cut to a particular length. First, DRAW a line on each piece, estimating where it will be cut. Then MEASURE using dimes, and DRAW a line in the correct place. How good was your estimate?

5 dimes

estimate measure

8 dimes

2 dimes

6 dimes

9 dimes

3 dimes

Measure Up

MEASURE the length of each object in inches.

HINT: *Inch* and *inches* are abbreviated as *in.*

1. 

in.

2. 
in.

3. 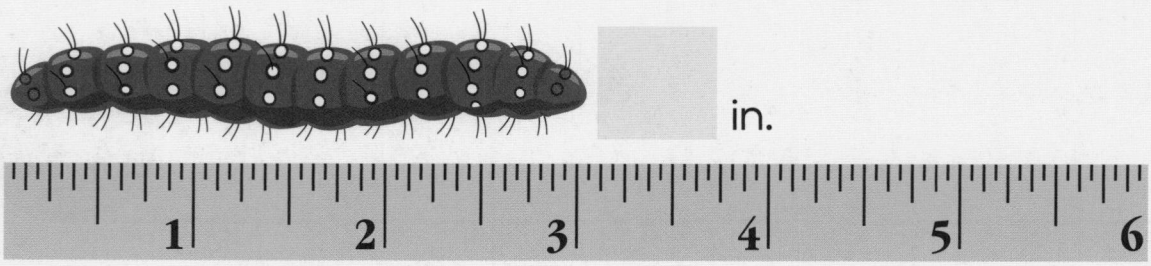

in.

4. 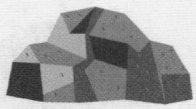
in.

5. 

in.

6. 
in.

Measure Up

MEASURE the approximate height of each flower in inches.

HINT: To find the approximate height, measure each flower and find the closest number on the ruler.

Rulers Rule

The candy at the top is 4 inches long. GUESS the length of each piece of candy in inches. Then MEASURE each one with a ruler to check your guess.

1. 

Guess: _____ in. Check: _____ in.

2. 

Guess: _____ in. Check: _____ in.

3. 

Guess: _____ in. Check: _____ in.

4. 

Guess: _____ in. Check: _____ in.

5. 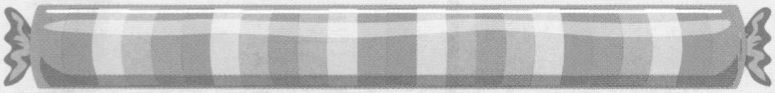

Guess: _____ in. Check: _____ in.

Rulers Rule

Each piece of yarn needs to be cut to a particular length. First, DRAW a line on each piece, estimating where it will be cut. Then MEASURE with a ruler, and DRAW a line in the correct place. How good was your estimate?

3 in.

1 in.

6 in.

4 in.

2 in.

5 in.

Measure Up

MEASURE the length of each ribbon in centimeters.

HINT: *Centimeter(s)* is abbreviated as *cm*.

1. 

cm

2. 

cm

3. 

cm

4. 

cm

5. 

cm

6. 

cm

Measure Up

MEASURE the approximate height of each action figure in centimeters.

Rulers Rule

The worm at the top is 10 centimeters long. GUESS the length of each worm in centimeters. Then MEASURE each worm with a ruler to check your guess.

1. 

Guess: _____ cm Check: _____ cm

2. 

Guess: _____ cm Check: _____ cm

3. 

Guess: _____ cm Check: _____ cm

4. 

Guess: _____ cm Check: _____ cm

5. 

Guess: _____ cm Check: _____ cm

Rulers Rule

Each piece of yarn needs to be cut to a particular length. First, DRAW a line on each piece, estimating where it will be cut. Then MEASURE with a ruler, and DRAW a line in the correct place. How good was your estimate?

6 cm

4 cm

2 cm

9 cm

7 cm

3 cm

Around We Go

Perimeter is the distance around a two-dimensional shape. WRITE the perimeter of each shape.

Example:

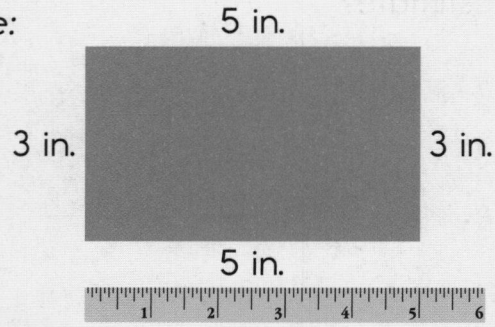

To find the perimeter, add the length of all of the sides.

5 + 3 + 5 + 3 = 16

The perimeter of this rectangle is 16 inches.

1.

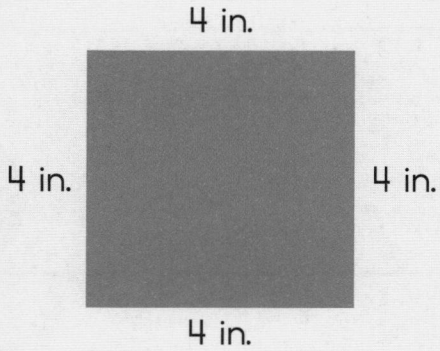

in.

2.

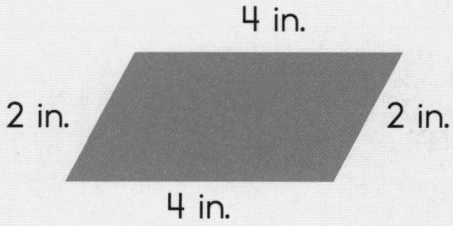

in.

3.

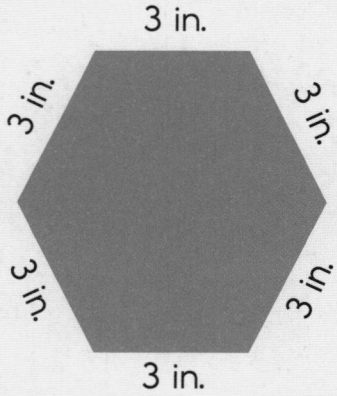

in.

4.

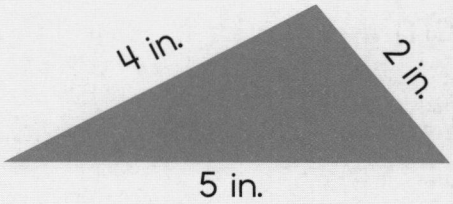

in.

Around We Go

MEASURE the length of each side of the shape in centimeters. Then WRITE the perimeter of the shape.

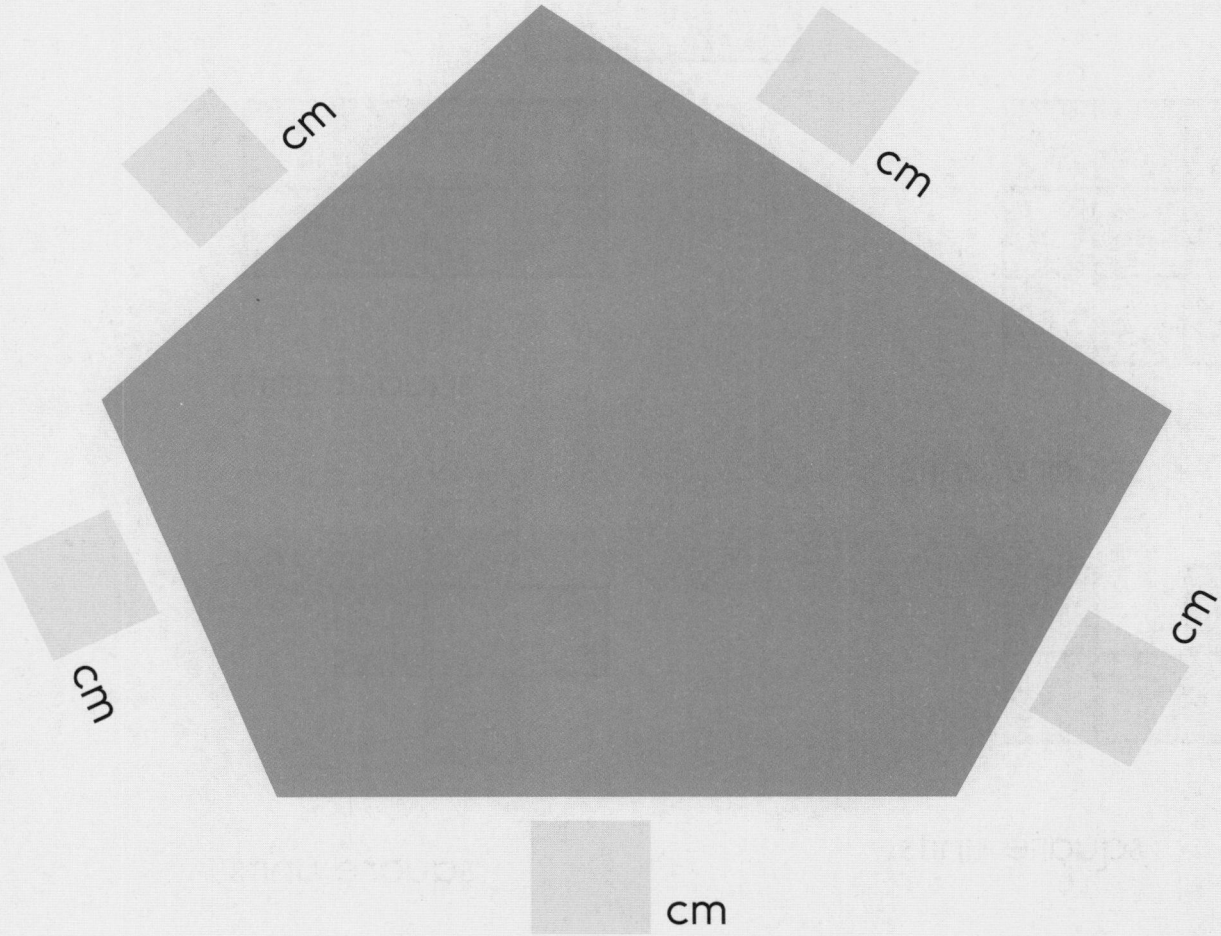

Perimeter: cm

Squared Away

Area is the size of the surface of a shape, and it is measured in square units.
WRITE the area of each shape.

Example:  1 square unit

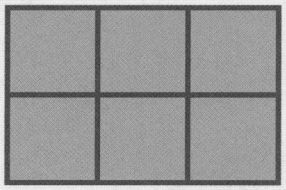

To measure the area, count the number of square units. The area of this rectangle is 6 square units.

1. 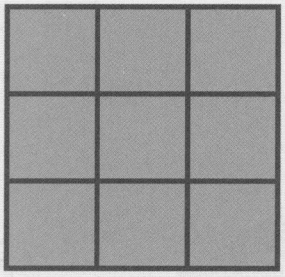

square units

2. 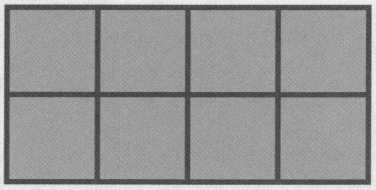

square units

3. 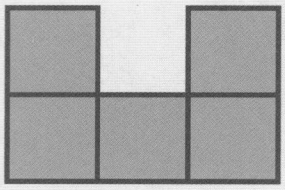

square units

4. 

square units

5. 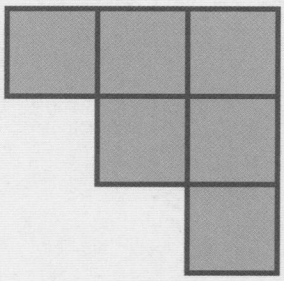

square units

6. 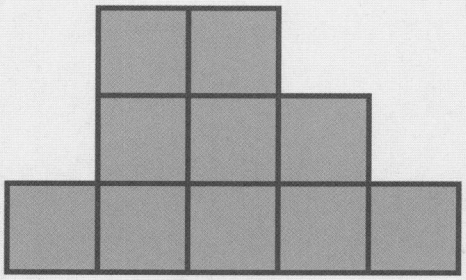

square units

Which One?

CIRCLE the shape that matches each area measurement.

1. 4 square units

2. 7 square units

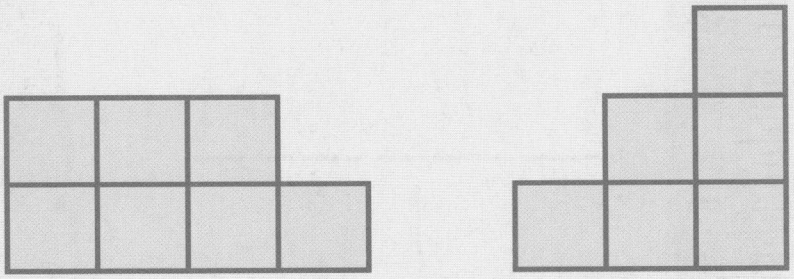

3. 5 square units

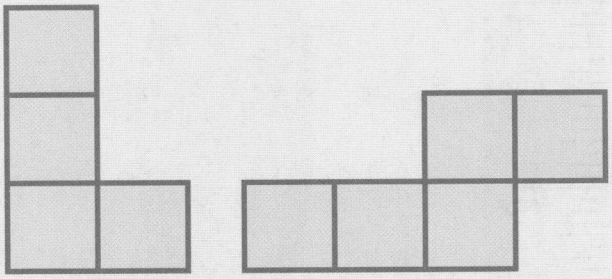

4. 6 square units

Work It Out

The Scrantonville Scouts just returned from their fishing trip at the lake. Sarah caught a fish that is 5 inches long. Willa caught a fish that is about 4 inches long. Jackie caught a fish measuring over 6 inches.

WRITE the name of each girl above her fish.

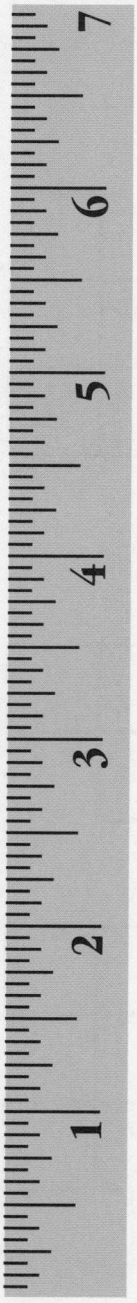

2. _____

1. _____

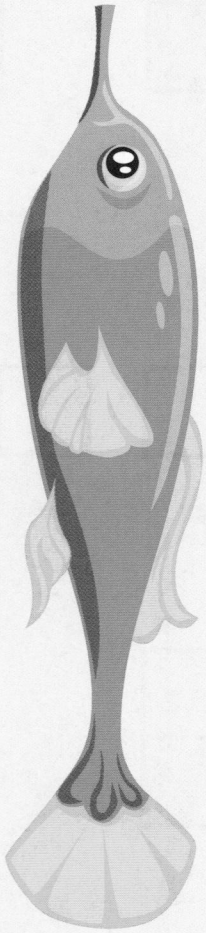

3. _____

Measure Up

WRITE the approximate length of each object in inches and centimeters.

1.

about ____ in. about ____ cm

2.

about ____ in. about ____ cm

3.

about ____ in. about ____ cm

4.

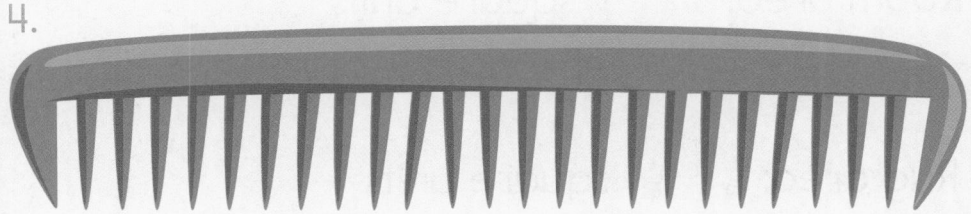

about ____ in.

about ____ cm

Work It Out

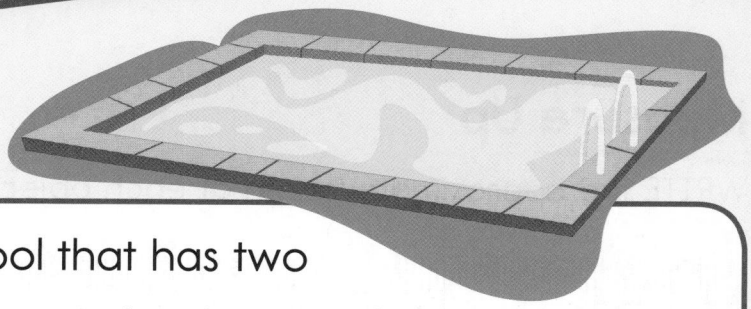

The Birnbaum family put in a pool that has two sides that are 12 feet long and two sides that are 8 feet long. The Jones family pool has two sides that are 15 feet long and two sides that are 7 feet long.

WRITE the perimeter of each pool, and CIRCLE the name of the family with the pool with the larger perimeter.

1. Birnbaum family: pool perimeter = _____ feet

2. Jones family: pool perimeter = _____ feet

Annie is trying to figure out how many rugs she can fit in her room. WRITE the area of the room and the tile. Then ANSWER the question.

Room:

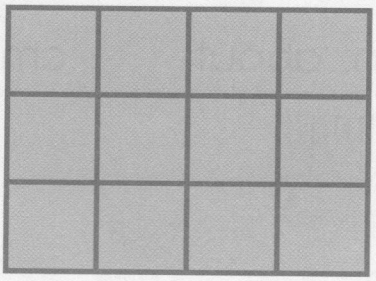

3. Room area: _____ square units

Rug:

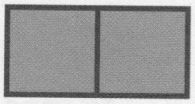

4. Rug area: _____ square units

5. What is the total number of rugs Annie will need to cover her floor? _____

Squared Away

WRITE the perimeter and area of each shape.

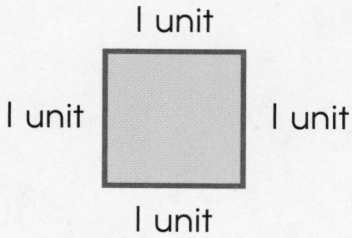

Perimeter: 4 units

Area: 1 square unit

1.

Perimeter: _____ units

Area: _____ square units

2.

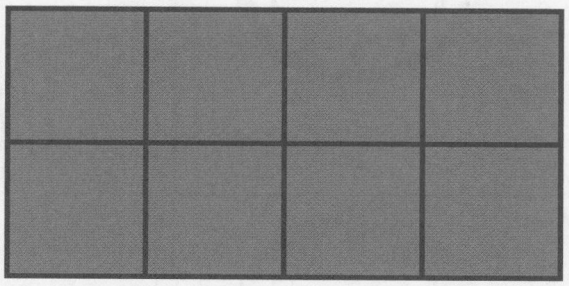

Perimeter: _____ units

Area: _____ square units

3.

Perimeter: _____ units

Area: _____ square units

4.

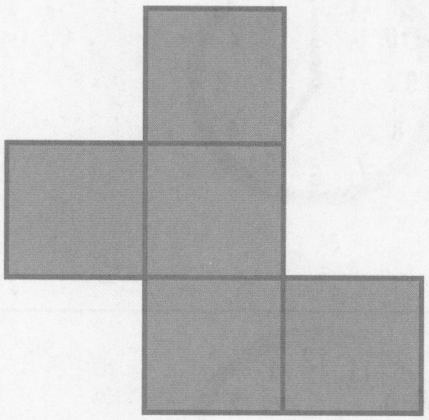

Perimeter: _____ units

Area: _____ square units

What Time Is It?

WRITE the time on each clock.

Examples:

4 : 00

8 : 30

1.

:

2.

:

3.

:

4.

:

5.

:

6.

:

Watch It!

DRAW a line to connect each watch to a clock that shows the same time.

Give Me a Hand

DRAW the clock hands to match the time.

1.

1:30

2.

4:00

3.

6:00

4.

8:30

5.

5:30

6.

3:00

7.

11:30

8.

7:30

Passing the Time

DRAW the time on the last clock to complete the pattern.

1.

2.

3.

4.

What Time Is It?

WRITE the time on each clock.

Examples:

1 : 15

5 : 45

1.

:

2.

:

3.

:

4.

:

5.

:

6.

:

Watch It!

DRAW a line to connect each watch to a clock that shows the same time.

Give Me a Hand

DRAW the clock hands to match the time.

1.

4:15

2.

12:45

3.

7:15

4.

1:45

5.

10:45

6.

5:15

7.

8:15

8.

2:45

Passing the Time

DRAW the time on the last clock to complete the pattern.

1.

2.

3.

4.

15-Minute Warning

Mom says you're leaving in 15 minutes.
WRITE the time you need to go.

1.

+ 15 minutes = ____ : ____

2.

+ 15 minutes = ____ : ____

3.

+ 15 minutes = ____ : ____

4.

+ 15 minutes = ____ : ____

Set Your Clock

Each clock is slow. DRAW hands to show the correct time on each clock.

HINT: Add time to each clock.

1.

2 hours slow →

2.

30 minutes slow →

3.

15 minutes slow →

4.

45 minutes slow →

Set Your Clock

Each clock is fast. DRAW hands to show the correct time on each clock.

HINT: Subtract time from each clock.

1.

15 minutes fast →

2.

3 hours fast →

3.

45 minutes fast →

4.

30 minutes fast →

Time Difference

WRITE the difference in time between each pair of clocks.

1.

hours minutes

2.

hours minutes

3.

hours minutes

4.

hours minutes

Save the Date

CIRCLE the correct answer.

Month

NOVEMBER						
S	M	T	W	T	F	S
	1	2	3	4	5	6
7	8	9	10	11	12	13
14	15	16	17	18	19	20
21	22	22	23	25	26	27
28	29	30				

Days of the week:
Sunday
Monday
Tuesday
Wednesday
Thursday
Friday
Saturday

1. What month is this?

   December July November

2. How many days are in this month?

   29 30 31

3. What is the first day of this month?

   Monday Thursday Saturday

4. What is the date of the first Friday?

   November 1 November 5 November 12

5. How many Mondays are in this month?

   3 4 5

6. How many Fridays are in this month?

   3 4 5

Save the Date

WRITE the correct answer.

JANUARY						
S	M	T	W	T	F	S
				1	2	3
4	5	6	7	8	9	10
11	12	13	14	15	16	17
18	19	20	21	22	23	24
25	26	27	28	29	30	31

FEBRUARY						
S	M	T	W	T	F	S
1	2	3	4	5	6	7
8	9	10	11	12	13	14
15	16	17	18	19	20	21
22	23	24	25	26	27	28

MARCH						
S	M	T	W	T	F	S
1	2	3	4	5	6	7
8	9	10	11	12	13	14
15	16	17	18	19	20	21
22	23	24	25	26	27	28
29	30	31				

APRIL						
S	M	T	W	T	F	S
			1	2	3	4
5	6	7	8	9	10	11
12	13	14	15	16	17	18
19	20	21	22	23	24	25
26	27	28	29	30		

MAY						
S	M	T	W	T	F	S
					1	2
3	4	5	6	7	8	9
10	11	12	13	14	15	16
17	18	19	20	21	22	23
24	25	26	27	28	29	30
31						

JUNE						
S	M	T	W	T	F	S
	1	2	3	4	5	6
7	8	9	10	11	12	13
14	15	16	17	18	19	20
21	22	23	24	25	26	27
28	29	30				

JULY						
S	M	T	W	T	F	S
			1	2	3	4
5	6	7	8	9	10	11
12	13	14	15	16	17	18
19	20	21	22	23	24	25
26	27	28	29	30	31	

AUGUST						
S	M	T	W	T	F	S
						1
2	3	4	5	6	7	8
9	10	11	12	13	14	15
16	17	18	19	20	21	22
23	24	25	26	27	28	29
30	31					

SEPTEMBER						
S	M	T	W	T	F	S
	1	2	3	4	5	
6	7	8	9	10	11	12
13	14	15	16	17	18	19
20	21	22	23	24	25	26
27	28	29	30			

OCTOBER						
S	M	T	W	T	F	S
				1	2	3
4	5	6	7	8	9	10
11	12	13	14	15	16	17
18	19	20	21	22	23	24
25	26	27	28	29	30	31

NOVEMBER						
S	M	T	W	T	F	S
1	2	3	4	5	6	7
8	9	10	11	12	13	14
15	16	17	18	19	20	21
22	23	24	25	26	27	28
29	30					

DECEMBER						
S	M	T	W	T	F	S
		1	2	3	4	5
6	7	8	9	10	11	12
13	14	15	16	17	18	19
20	21	22	23	24	25	26
27	28	29	30	31		

1. How many months are in one year? _____

2. What is the first month of the year? _____

3. Which month has 28 days? _____

4. How many months have 31 days? _____

5. What day of the week is Valentine's Day, February 14?

   _____

6. On what day of the week does October begin?

   _____

Save the Date

DRAW the pictures for the special events on the correct place on the calendar.

HINT: Some events last longer than one day.

Maya's beach party	July 17	
Florida vacation	July 30 to August 6	V
First day of school	August 31	1
Tyler's birthday	August 12	
Mom and Dad's anniversary	July 29	
Dad and Tyler's fishing trip	August 21–22	
Hota Dakota concert	July 3	
Dentist appointment	August 9	

JULY

Sunday	Monday	Tuesday	Wednesday	Thursday	Friday	Saturday
				1	2	3
4	5	6	7	8	9	10
11	12	13	14	15	16	17
18	19	20	21	22	23	24
25	26	27	28	29	30	31

AUGUST

Sunday	Monday	Tuesday	Wednesday	Thursday	Friday	Saturday
1	2	3	4	5	6	7
8	9	10	11	12	13	14
15	16	17	18	19	20	21
22	23	24	25	26	27	28
29	30	31				

What Time Is It?

WRITE the time on each clock.

1.

2.

3.

4.

5.

6.

7.

8.

Unit Rewind

WRITE the new time.

1. 

+ 45 minutes = ____ : ____

2. 

+ 15 minutes = ____ : ____

3. 

+ 30 minutes = ____ : ____

4. 

+ 45 minutes = ____ : ____

APRIL						
S	M	T	W	T	F	S
					1	2
3	4	5	6	7	8	9
10	11	12	13	14	15	16
17	18	19	20	21	22	23
24	25	26	27	28	29	30

5. How many days are in this month? _____

6. On what day of the week does this month begin? _____

7. What is the date of the first Wednesday?

_____

8. What day of the week is April 26?

_____

Which One?

CIRCLE the money that matches the dollar amount.

$1.42

$0.80

$1.23

$1.86

$2.06

$5.55

Match Up

DRAW lines to connect money with the same value.

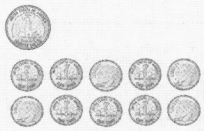

Money Bags

WRITE the value of the money on the bag.

1.

2.

3.

4.

5.

6.

Odd One Out

CROSS OUT the picture or number that does **not** match the others.

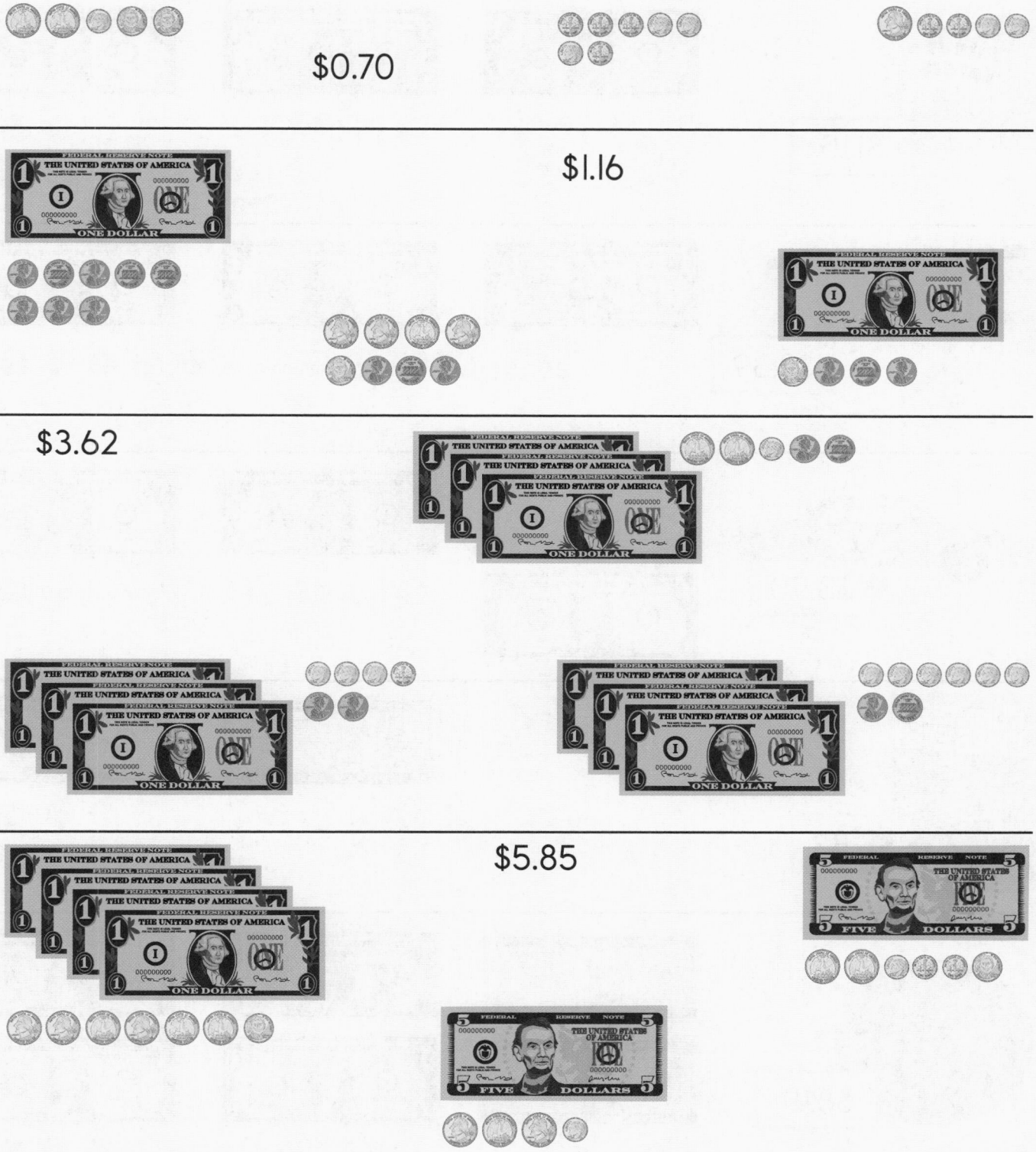

Pay Up

CIRCLE the money needed to buy each item using exact change.

$1.15

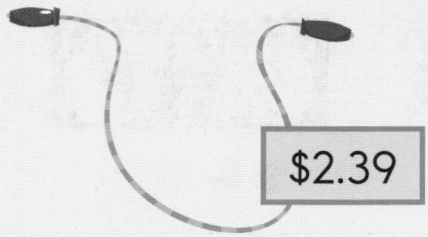

$2.39

$3.90

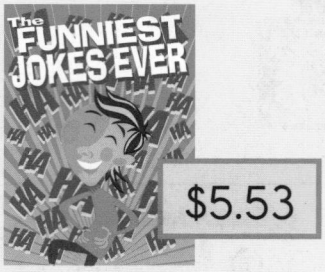

$5.53

$8.41

Match Up

DRAW lines to connect the money with the food that can be bought using exact change.

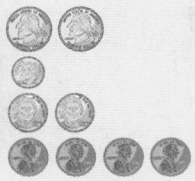

Who Can Buy It?

CIRCLE the hands of the people who have enough money to buy a movie ticket.

Pay Up

WRITE the cost to buy all three things.

Total cost $ _____ . _____

Circle It

CIRCLE all of the objects that cost **less** than the top object.

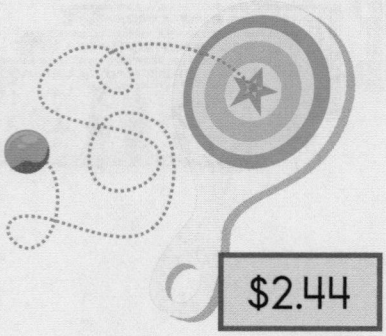

Matched or Mismatched?

WRITE >, <, or = in each box.

1.

2.

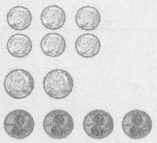

3.

4.

$2.99

5.

$4.02

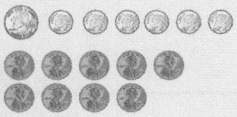

6.

$6.52

7.

$8.85

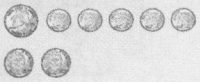

Money Bags

WRITE the value of the money on the bag.

1. $.

2. $.

3. $.

4. $.

5. $.

6. $.

Pay Up

CIRCLE the money needed to buy the soccer ball using exact change.

WRITE the cost to buy all three things.

Total cost $ ____ . ____

Which Is Less?

CIRCLE the picture with **less** money than the other.

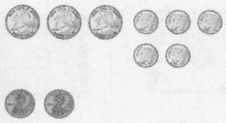

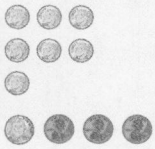

Mismatched

WRITE > or < in each box.

1. $0.13 ☐ $0.56

2. $5.44 ☐ $4.30

3. $2.69 ☐ $2.07

4. $5.21 ☐ $5.18

5. $8.25 ☐ $9.77

6. $3.32 ☐ $3.20

Page 126

1. 53
2. 25
3. 39
4. 17
5. 72
6. 81
7. 46
8. 68

Page 127

1. 16
2. 49
3. 83
4. 75
5. 58
6. 32
7. 94
8. 67

Page 128

1. 182
2. 433
3. 925
4. 657
5. 708

Page 129

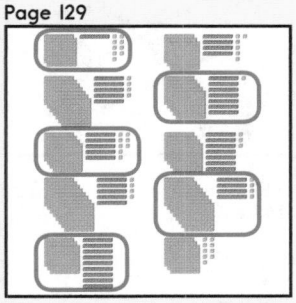

Page 130

1. one hundred sixty-two
2. three hundred seventy-four
3. two hundred fifty
4. eight hundred sixteen
5. six hundred forty-three
6. four hundred ninety-five

Page 131

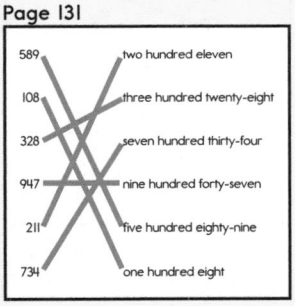

Pages 132–133

1	2	3	4	5	6	7	8	9	10
11	12	13	14	15	16	17	18	19	20
21	22	23	24	25	26	27	28	29	30
31	32	33	34	35	36	37	38	39	40
41	42	43	44	45	46	47	48	49	50
51	52	53	54	55	56	57	58	59	60
	62	63	64	65	66	67	68	69	70
71	72	73	74	75	76	77	78	79	80
81	82	83	84	85	86	87	88	89	90
91	92	93	94	95	96	97	98	99	100

Page 134

82	83	84	85	86	87	88	89
103	104	105	106	107	108	109	110
343	344	345	346	347	348	349	350
719	720	721	722	723	724	725	726
566	567	568	569	570	571	572	573
850	851	852	853	854	855	856	857

Page 135

234 235 236 237 238 239 240 241

981 982 983 984 985 986 987 988

97 98 99 100 101 102 103 104

874 875 876 877 878 879 880 881

699 700 701 702 703 704 705 706

395 396 397 398 399 400 401 402

Page 136

2 4 6 8 10 12 14 16

50 55 60 65 70 75 80 85

60 70 80 90 100 110 120 130

15 18 21 24 27 30 33 36

8 16 24 32 40 48 56 64

42 48 54 60 66 72 78 84

Page 137

66	68	70	72	74	76	78	80
20	30	40	50	60	70	80	90
15	20	25	30	35	40	45	50
27	30	33	36	39	42	45	48
62	66	70	74	78	82	86	90
42	49	56	63	70	77	84	91

Page 138

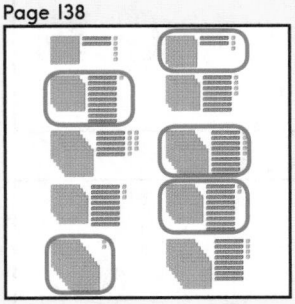

Page 139

1. 576
2. 329
3. 707
4. 458
5. 910

Page 140

1. <
2. >
3. <
4. >
5. <
6. <
7. >
8. <
9. >
10. >
11. >
12. <
13. <
14. >
15. <
16. >
17. <
18. >

Page 141

1. >
2. <
3. =
4. >
5. <
6. >
7. >
8. =

Page 142

1. 10
2. 20
3. 60
4. 70
5. 30
6. 40
7. 50
8. 60

Page 143

1. 700
2. 900
3. 400
4. 300
5. 500
6. 400
7. 200
8. 700
9. 300
10. 900
11. 700
12. 900

Page 144

Check:

1. 25
2. 160
3. 108

Page 145

Check:

1. 36
2. 17
3. 47

Page 146

1. 382, three hundred eighty-two
2. 740, seven hundred forty
3. 519, five hundred nineteen
4. 495, four hundred ninety-five
5. 906, nine hundred six

Page 147

245 246 247 248 249 250 251 252

589 590 591 592 593 594 595 596

724 725 726 727 728 729 730 731

40	45	50	55	60	65	70	75
26	29	32	35	38	41	44	47
11	17	23	29	35	41	47	53

Page 148

1. >
2. =
3. <
4. >
5. <
6. =
7. <
8. >
9. <

Page 149

1. 90
2. 30
3. 40
4. 60
5. 10
6. 100
7. 10
8. 20
9. 600
10. 200
11. 500
12. 700
13. 200
14. 400
15. 900
16. 200

17. Check: 58

Page 150

1. 56
2. 29
3. 78
4. 44
5. 68
6. 69

Page 151

1. 62
2. 96
3. 44
4. 89
5. 57
6. 79

Page 152

1. 79
2. 54
3. 98
4. 87
5. 44
6. 39
7. 76
8. 69
9. 77
10. 48
11. 31
12. 97
13. 59
14. 94
15. 64
16. 89

Page 153

1. 10
2. 21
3. 12
4. 45
5. 42
6. 65
7. 72
8. 18
9. 22
10. 13
11. 51
12. 43
13. 32
14. 31
15. 22
16. 12

Page 154

1. 43
2. 32
3. 52
4. 25
5. 13
6. 61

Page 155

1. 35
2. 31
3. 60
4. 12
5. 26
6. 41

Page 156

1. 27
2. 10
3. 21
4. 12
5. 81
6. 25
7. 62
8. 13
9. 40
10. 11
11. 30
12. 24
13. 52
14. 15
15. 72
16. 31

Answers

Page 157

1. 50	2. 46
3. 12	4. 15
5. 41	6. 20
7. 27	8. 21
9. 95	10. 34
11. 30	12. 69
13. 75	14. 24
15. 57	16. 48

Page 158

1. 42	2. 93
3. 82	4. 65
5. 91	6. 70

Page 159

1. 65	2. 92
3. 70	4. 81
5. 52	6. 73

Page 160

1. 61	2. 81
3. 90	4. 91
5. 70	6. 74
7. 35	8. 58
9. 32	10. 80
11. 66	12. 92

Page 161

1. 60	2. 75
3. 92	4. 67
5. 90	6. 41
7. 82	8. 50
9. 71	10. 64
11. 100	12. 95

Page 162

1. 67	2. 16
3. 39	4. 73
5. 18	6. 27

Page 163

1. 28	2. 18
3. 39	4. 66
5. 15	6. 57

Page 164

1. 59	2. 8
3. 29	4. 18
5. 38	6. 25
7. 26	8. 55
9. 37	10. 9
11. 28	12. 19

Page 165

1. 17	2. 4
3. 79	4. 57
5. 19	6. 38
7. 23	8. 41
9. 39	10. 47
11. 74	12. 9

Page 166

1. 22	2. 40
3. 45	4. 23
5. 56	6. 6

Page 167

1. 49
2. 44
3. 8
4. 12

Page 168

1. 61	2. 41
3. 20	4. 16
5. 79	6. 22
7. 44	8. 56
9. 89	10. 51
11. 15	12. 87

Page 169

1. 58	2. 39
3. 95	4. 89
5. 91	6. 81
7. 75	8. 64
9. 42	10. 33
11. 50	12. 21
13. 16	14. 14
15. 48	16. 29

Page 170

10

Page 171

8, 64

Page 172

1. 9	2. 6
3. 4	4. 3

Page 173

1. 4	2. 24
3. 12	4. 8

Page 174

1. 4
2. 6
3. 2

Page 175

4

Page 176

1. 3	2. 4
3. 7	4. 5

Page 177

1. 1, 2
2. 5, 3
3. 4, 2

Page 178

1. odd	2. even
3. odd	4. even
5. even	6. odd

Page 179

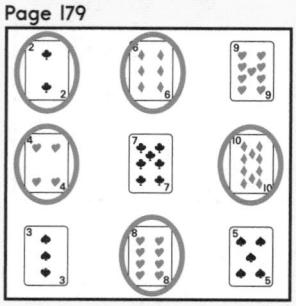

Page 180

1. 12	2. 8
3. 6	4. 4
5. 3	

Page 181

1. 9	2. odd
3. even	4. odd

Page 182

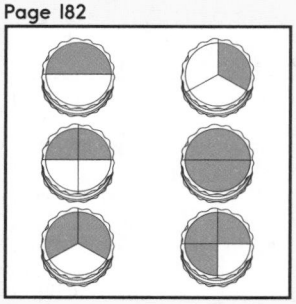

Page 183

1. $\frac{1}{4}$ 2. $\frac{1}{2}$ 3. $\frac{1}{3}$

4. $\frac{3}{4}$ 5. $\frac{3}{4}$ 6. $\frac{2}{2}$

Page 184

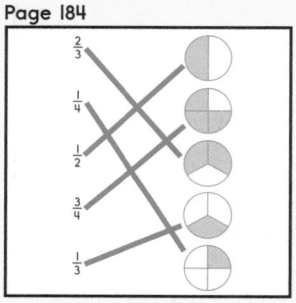

Page 185

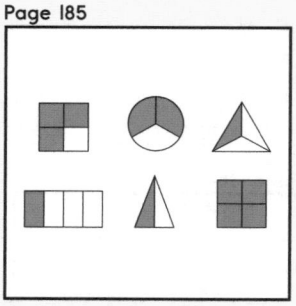

Page 186

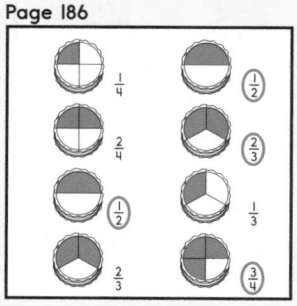

Page 187

1. $\frac{3}{4}$ $\frac{1}{2}$
2. $\frac{2}{3}$ $\frac{2}{2}$
3. $\frac{4}{4}$ $\frac{2}{3}$
4. $\frac{3}{4}$ $\frac{2}{4}$

Page 188

1. Ellie
2. Miles

Page 189

1. <	2. >
3. =	4. >
5. >	6. >
7. <	8. =
9. <	10. >
11. >	12. <

Page 190

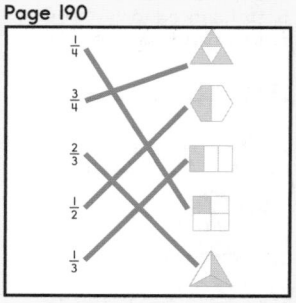

Page 191

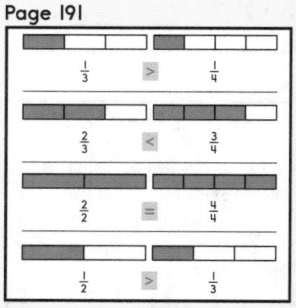

Page 192

1. 6
2. 3
3. 8
4. 4
5. 6
6. 2

Page 193
1. 7 2. 4
3. 3 4. 5
5. 6

Page 194
Check:
1. 7 2. 4
3. 9 4. 6
5. 8

Page 195
Ask someone to check your answers.

Page 196
1. 2 2. 5
3. 3 4. 1
5. 4 6. 3

Page 197
1. 5 2. 4
3. 7 4. 6

Page 198
Check:
1. 6 2. 3
3. 5 4. 2
5. 4

Page 199
Ask someone to check your answers.

Page 200
1. 4 2. 8
3. 5 4. 10
5. 2 6. 6

Page 201
1. 13 2. 11
3. 15 4. 12

Page 202
Check:
1. 7 2. 14
3. 8 4. 12
5. 16

Page 203
Ask someone to check your answers.

Page 204
1. 16 2. 12
3. 18 4. 11

Page 205

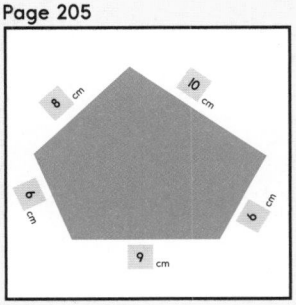

Perimeter: 39 cm

Page 206
1. 9 2. 8
3. 5 4. 5
5. 6 6. 10

Page 207

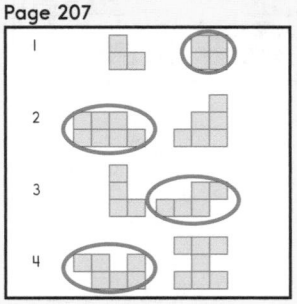

Page 208
1. Sarah
2. Jackie
3. Willa

Page 209
1. 2, 5 2. 4, 10
3. 6, 15 4. 5, 13

Page 210
1. 40
2. 44 [Jones circled]
3. 12
4. 2
5. 6

Page 211
1. 8, 4 2. 12, 8
3. 12, 6 4. 12, 5

Page 212
1. 1:30 2. 10:00
3. 5:00 4. 12:30
5. 2:30 6. 7:00

Page 213

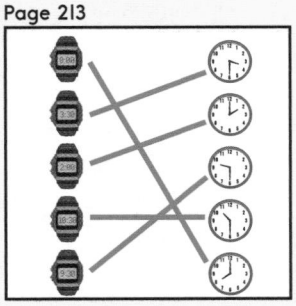

Page 214

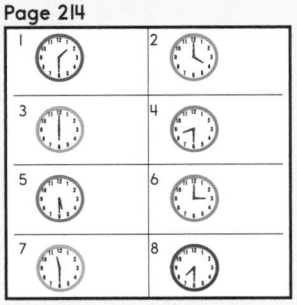

Page 215

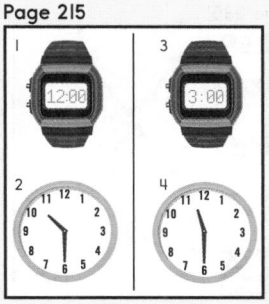

Page 216
1. 3:45 2 12:15
3. 10:15 4. 4:45
5. 8:45 6. 10:15

Page 217

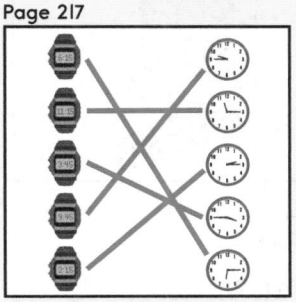

Page 218

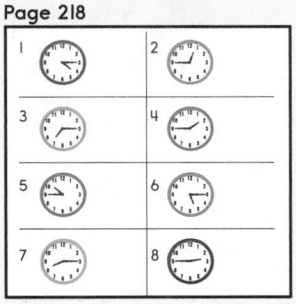

Page 219

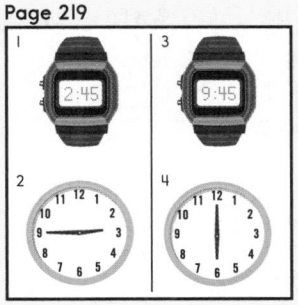

Page 220
1. 2:15 2. 11:45
3. 4:00 4. 6:30

Page 221

Page 222

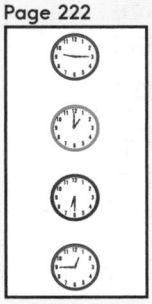

Page 223
1. 3 hours 30 minutes
2. 2 hours 15 minutes
3. 4 hours 30 minutes
4. 4 hours 15 minutes

Page 224
1. November
2. 30
3. Monday
4. November 5
5. 5
6. 4

Page 225
1. 12
2. January
3. February
4. 7
5. Saturday
6. Thursday

Page 226–227

Page 228
1. 3:30 2. 12:15
3. 8:45 4. 4:00
5. 5:15 6. 2:45
7. 9:45 8. 6:30

Answers

Page 229

1. 12:45
2. 6:00
3. 8:00
4. 2:30
5. 30
6. Friday
7. April 6
8. Tuesday

Page 230

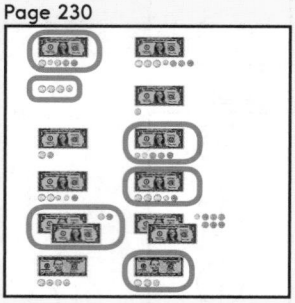

Page 231

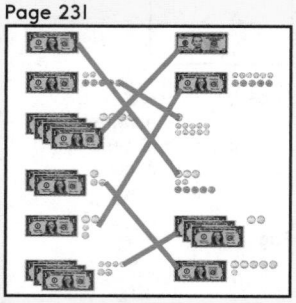

Page 232

1. $0.82
2. $1.41
3. $2.35
4. $2.11
5. $5.47
6. $7.00

Page 233

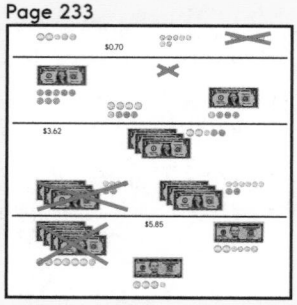

Page 234

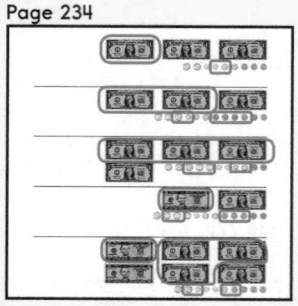

Page 235

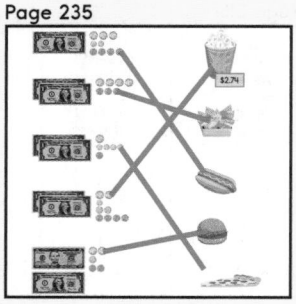

Page 236

Page 237

$27.97

Page 238

Page 239

1. >
2. <
3. =
4. <
5. >
6. <
7. =

Page 240

1. $1.71
2. $6.22
3. $5.20
4. $9.04
5. $10.98
6. $13.07

Page 241

$15.09

Page 242

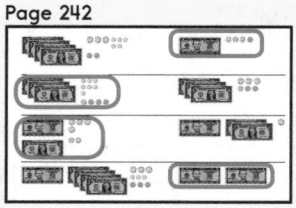

1. <
2. >
3. >
4. >
5. <
6. >

Sylvan for Every Student!

SINGLE-SUBJECT WORKBOOKS

- ☑ Focus on individual skills and subjects
- ☑ Fun activities and grade-appropriate exercises

3-IN-1 SUPER WORKBOOKS

- ☑ Three Sylvan single-subject workbooks in one package for just $18.99!
- ☑ Perfect practice for the student who needs to focus on a range of topics

FUN ON THE RUN ACTIVITY BOOKS

- ☑ Just $3.99/$4.75 Can.
- ☑ Colorful games and activities for on-the-go learning

FLASHCARD SETS

- ☑ Spelling and vocabulary for Pre-K–5th grade
- ☑ Math for Pre-K–5th grade

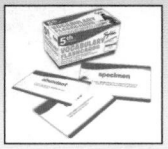

PAGE PER DAY WORKBOOKS

- ☑ Perforated pages—perfect for your child to do just one workbook page each day
- ☑ Extra practice the easy way!

KICK START PACKAGES

- ☑ Includes books, flashcards, access to online activities, and more
- ☑ Everything your child needs in one comprehensive package

Try FREE pages today at SylvanPagePerDay.com

1000

Sylvan Learning

SPECIAL OFFER FROM Sylvan Learning℠

Congratulations on your Sylvan product purchase! Your child is now on the way to building skills for academic success. Sylvan would like to extend a special offer for a discount on our exclusive Sylvan Skills Assessment® to you and your family. Bring this coupon to your scheduled assessment to receive your discount. Limited time offer.* One per family.

You are entitled to a $10 DISCOUNT on a Sylvan Skills Assessment®.

It includes a comprehensive evaluation of your child's needs using our unique combination of standardized tests, teacher observations, and personal interviews. This assessment is the key to creating a personal learning plan just for your child, targeting those exact skills your child needs.

Visit SylvanLearningProducts.com/coupon today to find a participating location and schedule your Sylvan Skills Assessment®.

CUT ALONG THE DOTTED LINE

* Offer expires December 31, 2014. Valid at participating locations.
Offer will be valued at local currency equivalent on date of registration with Sylvan Learning.

Moms, Dads, Teachers, and Homeschoolers Give Rave Reviews!

"**Samantha loves these books** because to her, they are not schoolwork. They are fun activities. But really she is learning, and doing the same work she does at school."

—MommyMandy.com

"As an early childhood teacher, I know that good reading, vocabulary, and spelling skills make an essential foundation for both academic success as well as lifelong learning. **Sylvan Learning Workbooks & Learning Kits** are an awesome resource that I'd have no problem recommending to the parents of any of my students who are struggling."

—TheOpinionatedParent.com

"As a teacher, I look for different aspects in a resource than a student or a parent might. . . . **The book has vibrant, attractive colors, and the worksheets are really fun.** My 10-year-old son has been enjoying them since I got the book. . . . I recommend this book to students, parents, and teachers alike for increasing student achievement."

—DynamiteLessonPlan.com

"If you are looking for some **good, fun learning books for your child**, I definitely recommend the Sylvan Learning series."

—TheDadJam.com